WWII US ARMY
IN EUROPE AND THE PACIFIC

JAVIER REDONDO

Painting and weathering AFVs
with Vallejo products

WWII US Army in Europe and Pacific
Painting and weathering AFV with Vallejo products

Author
Javier Redondo Giménez

Direction and development
Acrylicos Vallejo, S.L.

Design and layout
Acrylicos Vallejo, S.L.

Editing
Acrylicos Vallejo, S.L.

Photography
Javier Redondo Giménez

Painter
Javier Redondo Giménez

Profiles
Pablo Patricio Albornoz

Publihsher
Acrylicos Vallejo, S.L.

ISBN
978-84-09-18821-5

Legal Deposit
B 11023-2021

Printer in Spain
Nueva Imprenta, S.L.

CONTENT

WWII US ARMY IN EUROPE & THE PACIFIC

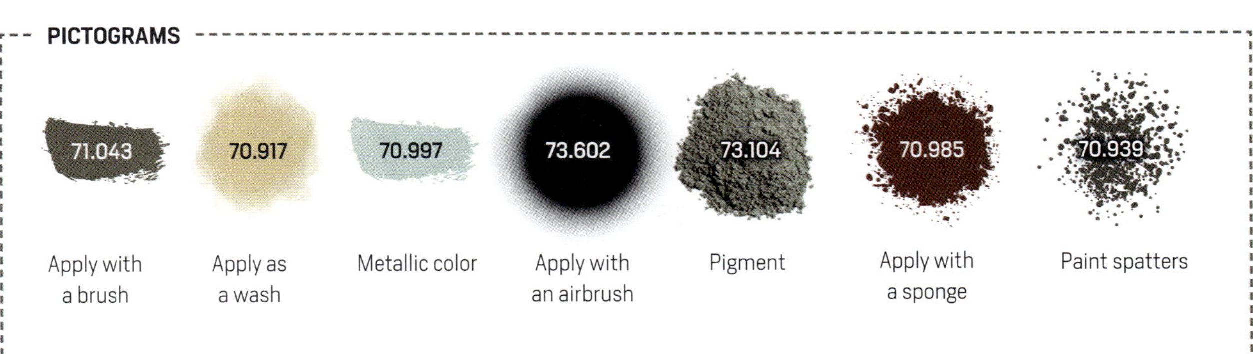

BIOGRAPHY

Javier Redondo

When I was twelve years old, I began to glue pieces of plastic together and paint them, trying to end up with something which would sort of look like a model. My first efforts were not too auspicious and as far as leaning towards one theme or another, I treated ships, planes and tanks alike. The only determining factor in my choice of subject was if I could afford to buy the kit or not.

Some years later I started to lean towards military vehicles, mainly because of the range of Esci models available in 1/72 scale and their attractive box art, and the Matchbox range in 1/76 scale, which also included a scenic base and came with "everything included". Since then I have retained this preferences for vignettes and dioramas, which I consider to be the pinnacle of modeling and the ultimate expression of our hobby.

My first model in 1/35 scale was a Panzer I Ausf B from Italeri, which I still remember with great affection. The level of detail on that model amazed me and led me to the conclusion that this would be the most fitting scale to realise my modeling aspirations. Although in the intervening years I have occasionally touched on other scales, most of my work tends to be in 1/35.

My modeling interests focus upon the Great War and the Second World War, and I am certain that these historical periods continue to fascinate me because they allow me to combine my two pastimes, history and painting.

In these periods, which I do not stray from unless told to do so by a "judicial order", my interests incline towards the vehicles and tanks of the Spanish Civil War and towards material used by the Soviet Union in WWII. I am especially fascinated by the T-34 in all its forms and variations.

When starting a project, I like to collect as much pictorial reference material as I can to help me with the details of the model, and especially all the historical reference, so that I know the where, how and when of my model and, in particular, the particular exterior features I need to reproduce. It is of great importance for me to know the location of my subject, as this will clearly affect the build of the model and especially the final weathering effects portrayed.

With respect to the build, I must say that I find it difficult to build a model "from the box". I always end up complicating things with some level of detailing, a transformation or improvement which adds that personal touch to the model which I find very pleasing, although I must admit that I that enjoy painting the model more than building it.

When the time comes to paint the model, my personal preference is to depict vehicles that have been burnt out or wrecked in battle. I enjoy enormously the reproduction of different effects such as mud, dust and grease, as well as all those details which in the end bring individuality to a model. And as a final touch I enjoy placing the model on a terrain or diorama which explains and provides its context and history.

Pablo Patricio Albornoz

Pablo Albornoz was born in Nogoyá, Entre Rios, in Argentina, and began his career as an artist in the field of aviation in 2013. Within a short time, his paintings were on display in Latin American museums and institutions, as well as in foreign embassies, while his work was acquired by EEUU and European collections.

Due to his participation in exhibitions such as in The National Senate in Argentina, in 2017 he began an incursion into digital art, adding naval illustration and science fiction to his themes, and, more recently, branching out into tanks and armoured vehicles of all periods.

INTRODUCTION

BY JAVIER REDONDO

During the course of WWII, the US Engineer Corps, which was responsible for the camouflage of all the US Army material, developed a large number of bulletins, field manuals and diverse technical guides. These were used to instruct the Engineer Camouflage Battalions and may also have been supplied to other units, where they were probably ignored. The two most important editions were the FM 5-20 and FMN 5-21, which were issued in October 1942.

All through the war, the US engineer battalions used the 12 colors available for the camouflage and concealment of the equipment, colors which are listed below by name, number and Federal Standard and Methuen equivalent.

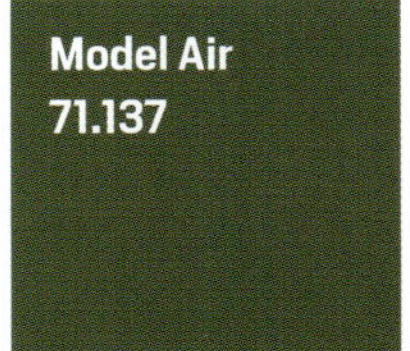

No. 1 Light Green
34151/30E8

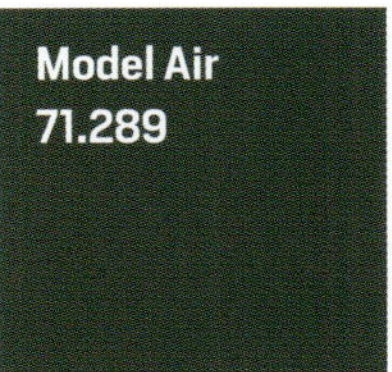

No. 2 Dark Green
34102/30F5

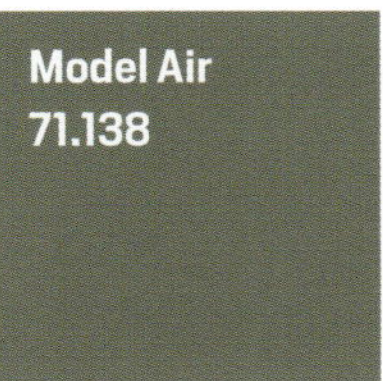

No. 3 Sand
30277/5C3

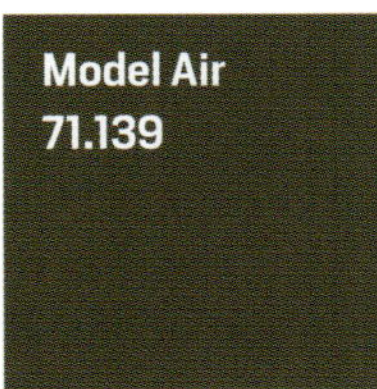

No. 4 Field Drab
30118/5E4

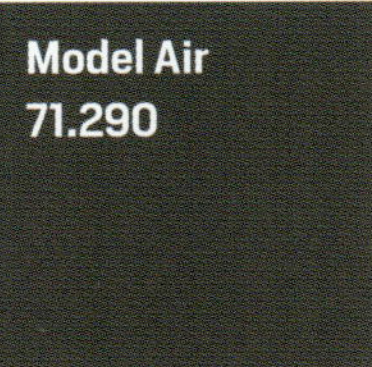

No. 5 Earth Brown
30099/6F5

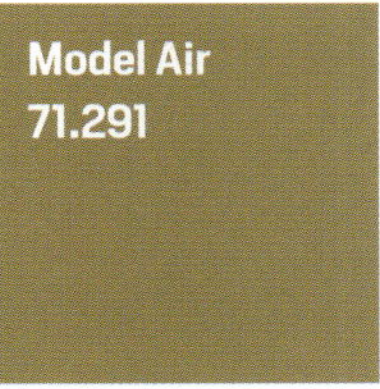

No. 6 Earth Yellow
30257/5D7

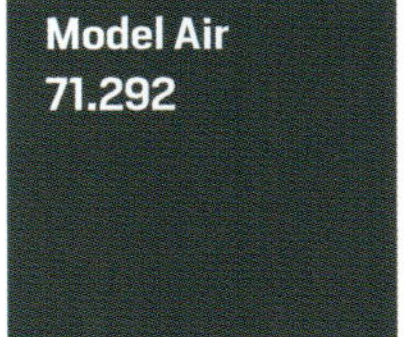

No. 7 Loam
34086/5F3

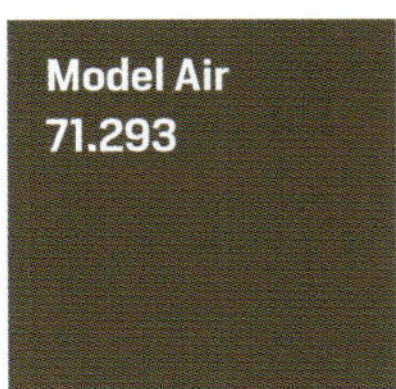

No. 8 Earth Red
30117/7E6

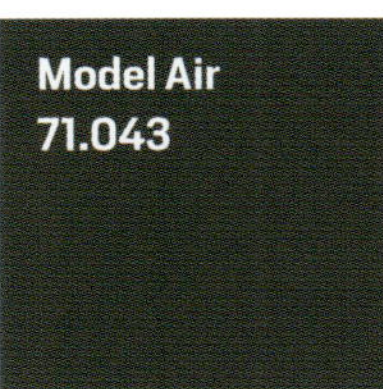

No. 9 Olive Drab
34087/4F4

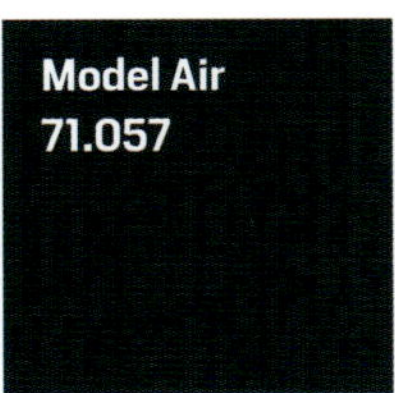

No. 10 Black
37038

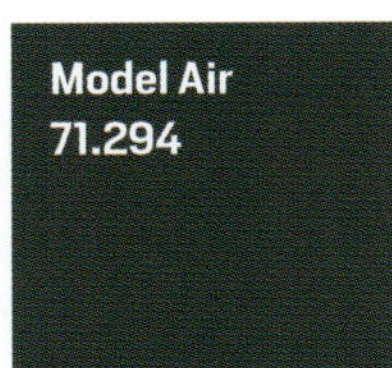

No. 11 Forest Green
34079/30F4

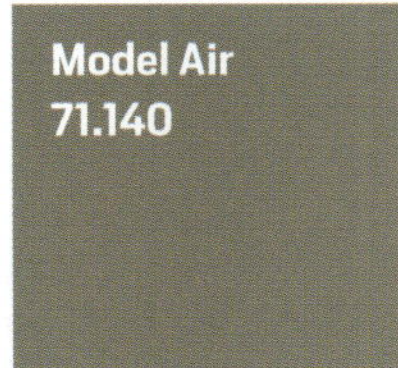

No. 12 Desert Sand
30279/7C4

In the field of military modeling, a general belief exists that the vehicles the US developed during WWII were boring because they were always painted in Olive Drab, this however is not true. Throughout the war, different patterns of camouflage were tried out to break the outline of the tanks, not so much for fear of airborne enemy attacks, which were quickly neutralized by the Allied forces, but to distract the land forces of the enemy, which were armed with powerful guns capable of destruction at a distance which the Allied forces could not equal. A study of the black-and-white photographs of the era is of little help, because the scale of greys tends to unify the various shades of color into one. Only in very detailed sharp photographs can we see that in fact two, three and up to four colors were used.

With the models on the following pages we try to give an overview of the entire war, showing some of the camouflage patterns deployed by the US Army during the conflict.

M3 STUART USMC

GUADALCANAL BATTLE, SOLOMON ISLANDS, 1942

After the Japanese attack on Pearl Harbor, on December 7th, 1941, and the following declaration of war by Italy and Germany on the 11th of that same month, the US Army had to bring the troops to immediate fighting readiness to face a war on two fronts.

During the first months of the war, the situation in the Pacific went from one disaster to another, there seemed to be no way of stopping the Imperial Japanese Army in its advances and conquests. The US Army lacked the experience which the enemy had gathered by fighting in China and Korea.

Finally, Guadalcanal was to be the turning point. At first the US Army and Marine Corps resisted the Japanese thrust and then, in a long battle that lasted from August 1942 to February 1943, they defeated and expelled the Japanese forces from the island.

In this campaign, the 1st Marine Division would use the obsolete M2 tank and the light M3 Stuart. These tanks originally belonged to the US Army and were issued in the standard OD Olive Drab No 9 FS34087/4F4, common to all the land vehicles of the era. The Marines painted yellow stripes around the turrets and, as the campaign developed, the crews started adding improvised camouflage, usually lines in light brown and yellow tones, applied in irregular patterns.

The Stuart tank we are going to build was used by the Marines in the assault of the powerful Gifu Line, during the Guadalcanal offensive of January 10th, 1943, which was aimed to occupy Mount Austen and the two nearby hills known as Seahorse and Galloping Horse. After fierce fighting, on January 23rd, the three objectives were reached, leaving more than 3000 dead Japanese soldiers in the field.

M3 STUART USMC

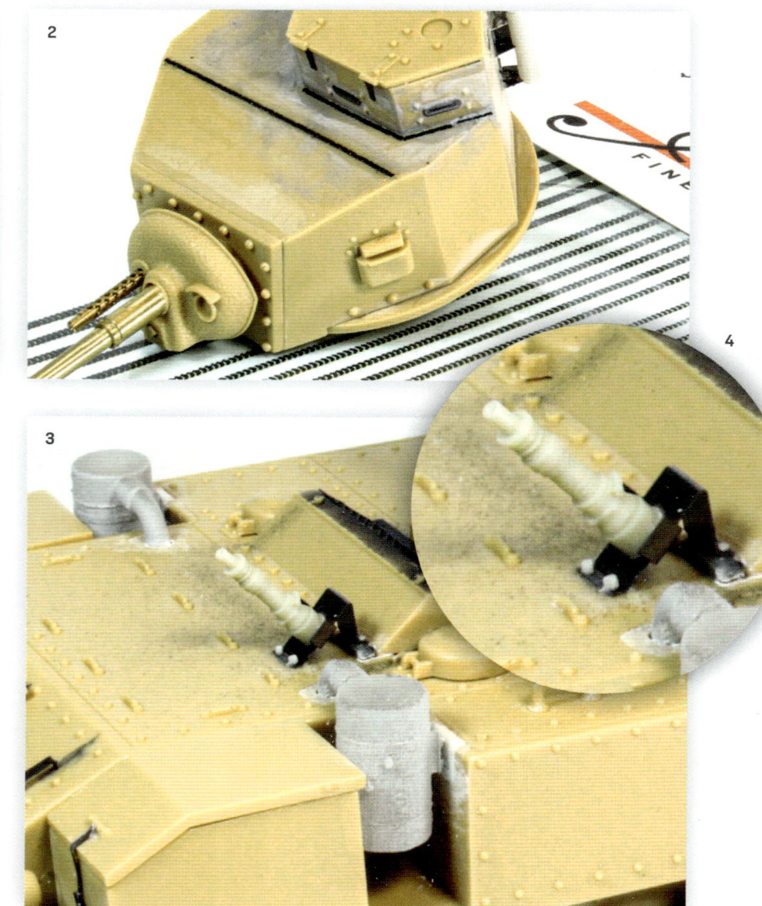

1 For this job, we will use Academy's Stuart "Honey", reference 13270, which includes the early turret that we need. This kit is good value for money and allows for an easy build without particular problems.

2 The turret had neither the welds lines that join together the two horizontal plates nor the ones that connect those with the hatch. To make these, the Archer tridimensional weld decals were used and provided an excellent result.

MATERIALS USED

- Eduard 35502 "M3 Stuart Honey" photo-etch set
- Orange Hobby G35-040 "37 mm M6 barrel" kit
- RB Model 35B082 "7,62 mm Browning M1919" kit
- FC Modeltrend 35500 "M3 Stuart Details" set
- M4 Models 35017 "Antenna allied bases"

3 The air filters of the kit were replaced by some with better details, 3D printed by FC Modeltrend.

4 The support of the antenna was made with a photo-etched part, two rivets and a resin antenna base made by M4 Models.

5 For the brackets, straps and moorings of the tools, the photo-etch set was used again. The shovel was a spare bit from another kit that fitted perfectly.

6 The tool boxes were detailed with photo-etched straps and included a piece of plastic on their lower side. Also, the missing line of rivets was added on the cover of the tracks.

7 The worst part of the kit were the wheels of the running gear, with scarce detailing and not-too-correct intersections between the spokes. These were changed for the wheels of the old Stuart Tamiya kit.

8 The headlamps were hollowed out so that some lenses for detailing could be inserted. Their covers had to be replaced by photo-etched covers in order to get the correct fineness required by the scale.

9 The front hatches have the gap for the visor, so the glass was reproduced with a bit of acetate glued in the inside and painted in bluish green.

10 The addition of the Browning machineguns and the 37 mm cannon. The turned metal barrel provides a level of detail which would be hard to improve.

11 The bracket for the outer machinegun was made with brass pipe and plastic.

TRACKS

12 Starting with the vinyl tracks, the rubber tread T16 tracks were primed with Surface Primer Black 73.602.

13 Both sides were painted with Track Primer 70.304, thinned with some drops of Airbrush Thinner 71.261.

14 On both sides where the bolts and teeth are located, Dark Rust Wash 76.507 and Light Rust Wash 76.505 were airbrushed successively.

15 The central part of the rubber treads was lightened with an airbrushed wash of Pale Grey 73.202.

16 In the same way, washes were applied over the surfaces of the tracks with Desert Dust Wash 76.522 and Sepia 73.200.

17 Using Black Wash 73.201 a blurred line was drawn in the central part of the rubber threads.

18 The tracks were finished by dry-brushing some Silver 70.997 over the edges of the teeth, to simulate that they had been polished by friction with the running gear.

19 After washing the kit properly with warm water and soap in order to remove any dirt caused by handling and building, a primer coat was airbrushed with Grey 73.601 , to provide a good base for the paint job to follow.

20 Next comes the tank itself, starting with the yellow stripe on the turret because it is easier to work first on the light tones than the dark ones. Deep Yellow 70.915 was used, muted down a bit with some Mud Brown 71.037.

21 Once dry, the area that the stripe would occupy was masked with masking tape and the basecoat was applied. When the basecoat was dry, the tape was removed leaving a perfectly defined yellow stripe.

22 The olive green tone was made with US Olive Drab 71.043 with a bit of Deep Yellow 70.915 airbrushed in thin layers until the entire model was covered.

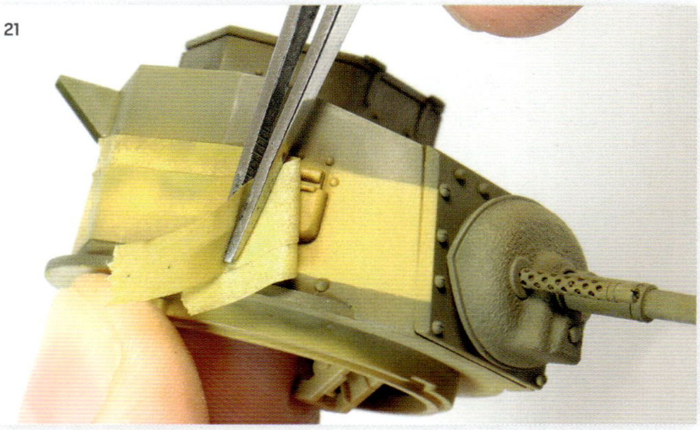

23 The rubber wheels of the running gear were painted with Dark Rubber 70.306.

24 Next, the lower part of the tank was worked on with a selection of ochre, brown and white oils. Bits of color were added over a surface previously dampened with White Spirit.

25 With a flat brush the shades are blended in vertical strokes to get diverse translucent tonalities.

26 The points of the running gear which are in contact with the teeth of the tracks are polished with a blending stump and graphite powder

27 Finally the tracks, now painted and weathered, are fitted and the lower part was done. Working this way is more comfortable and it avoids handling afterwards, which is always risky when a kit is almost finished.

27

28 With a mix of Ivory 71.075 and Khaki Brown 71.024 the various panels and surfaces were made a bit lighter.

29

30

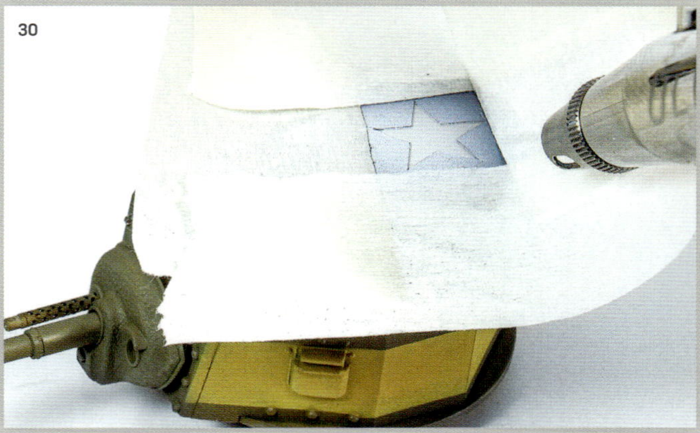

29 The air recognition badge of the hatch, a white five-pointed star, was made with an adhesive template fixed in place.

30 Next several coats of Insignia White 71.279 were airbrushed at low pressure.

31 The template mask was carefully removed and the white star was done.

31

MASKING: STAR

M3 STUART USMC

32 To accentuate the wear on the OD, some filters with Dark Yellow Wash 76.503 and Sepia 73.200 were added.

33 After that, a subtle dry-brushing with Buff 70.976 was applied on the rivets and screws.

34 USMC license plates for vehicles and armour were painted in yellow, they were applied using an Archer transfer sheet, specially designed for that purpose.

35 The shapes, details and contours were enhanced by using a controlled wash with a mix of Oiled Earth 76.521 and Blue Grey 76.524.

36 Working area after area, bits of color were added over a surface previously dampened with white spirit. In the horizontal parts, the color was blended with a circular motion of the brush, and in the vertical ones with vertical strokes.

37 Even if the US Olive Drab color is sometimes regarded as "boring", it can be applied with different tonalities to achieve an attractive chromatic richness.

38 With a pencil, a graphite bar and a blending stump, the metallic effects were incorporated in a rational and logical way, taking care not to overdo it.

M3 STUART USMC
DUST & DIRT

39 Dust and dirt effects are achieved with pigments applied with a brush.

40 The effects are applied in areas of choice, blurring carefully the edges of the application.

41 Pigment Binder 26.233 is applied using capillary action over the previous pigments. This product softens the effects and provides a greater adherence to the pigments.

39

40

41

42 Oiled Earth 76.521 was used to simulate the splashes.

43 Spilled oil around the tanks' filler caps was simulated by using a brush and Fuel Stains 73.814.

44 The rear pilot lights were painted with Transparent Red 70.934.

45 In the rear access compartments to the motor block, oil stains were applied with Oil Stains 73.813.

46 The process was finished by applying Rain Marks 73.819 and Petrol Spills 73.817.

M3 STUART USMC

WEATHERING

COLOR CHART

Tracks:
Priming: Black 73.602
Base: Track Primer 70.304
Rust washes:
Dark Rust 76.507
Light Rust 76.505
Highlights:
Pale Grey 73.202
Washes:
Desert Dust 76.522
Sepia 73.200
Black 73.201
Metallic: Silver 70.997

Wheels:
Dark Rubber 70.306

Camouflage:
Priming: Grey 73.601
Yellow stripe:
Deep Yellow 70.915
Mud Brown 71.037
Base: Deep Yellow 70.915
US Olive Drab 71.043

Pilot:
Transparent Red 70.934

Star:
Insignia White 71.279

Weathering:
Filters:
Ivory 71.075
Khaki Brown 71.024
Dark Yellow 76.503
Sepia 73.200
Drybrush:
Buff 70.976
Oil & grease:
Oiled Earth 76.521
Blue Grey 76.524
Fuel Stains 73.814
Oil Stains 73.813
Rain Marks 73.819
Petrol Spills 73.817
Dust & dirt
Light Yellow Ochre 73.102
Light Slate Grey 73.113
Light Sienna 73.104
Dark Red Ochre 73.107
Pigment Binder 26.233
Splashes
Oiled Earth 76.521

WEATHERING
73.107
73.102
73.104
73.113
Dust & dirt
CAMOUFLAGE
70.915
+
71.037
70.915
+
71.043
73.601
Priming
Yellow stripe
Base
STAR
71.279
U.S.M.C.
60180
70.306
WHEELS
73.602
70.304
73.202
76.507
76.505
76.522
73.200
73.201
70.997
Priming
Base
Highlights
Rust washes
Washes
Metallic
TRACKS

DODGE WC55 37 MM M6 ANTI-TANK

TUNISIA, 1943

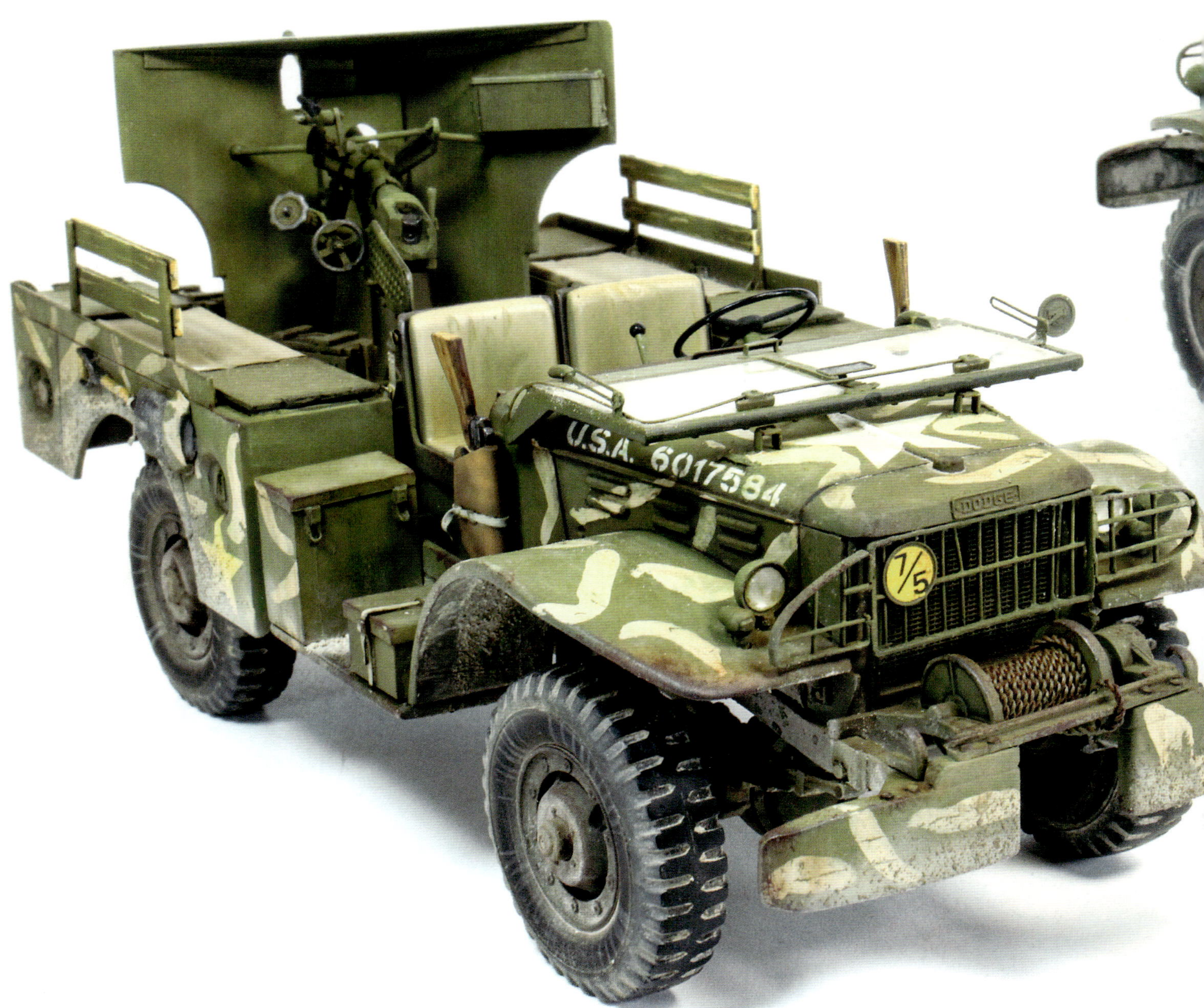

The US Army had baptism of fire during Operation Torch in North Africa, when they landed in Morrocco and Algeria, countries loyal to the collaborationist French Vichy government. The US troops reached their planned objectives against an inconsistent resistance by the French troops who finally disposed of their weapons and switched to the Allied side, helping their way to a quick advance through Algeria and Tunisia.

But as yet the German occupation troops were not going to give way easily. The first important clash with the German defenders was at the Battle of Kasserine Pass, where the inexperienced and ill-commanded American troops suffered a humiliating defeat with huge losses of men and material.

The superior weaponry and experience of the German troops were of large technical and psychological consequences for the Americans, even though they were able to recover quickly thanks to the rapid and continuous supply of material.

Upon disembarking on the continent, the American material which landed in Africa had no camouflage at all and once the fighting with the Germans started, the urgent necessity of camouflage became immediately evident since the vehicles were painted with the dark Olive Drab No. 9 FS34087/4F4, a color that made them stand out against the pale background of the desert. As the required paint was not available in sufficient quantities, most of the vehicles were camouflaged on the field and frequently mud was used for the desert color schemes.

The Dodge WC 55 was a modification of the versatile light truck Dodge WC52. It was armed with a 37 mm anti-tank gun, and designated to serve as an infantry support and as a self-propelled anti-tank weapon. The troops which had been issued this vehicle disliked it, it lacked armour and, as they soon learned in Tunisia, the 37 mm gun was obsolete and useless against the German armour of the period.

After this campaign, the guns were removed from many of these vehicles and they were reused as cargo trucks; the rest disappeared gradually from the frontlines as soon as 75 and 76 mm armored anti-tank weapons became available.

DODGE WC55 37 MM M6 ANTI-TANK

MATERIALS USED

- Limes 35019 "Grill for Dodge Beep" detail set
- Eduard 35403 "WC-51 Beep Weapons Carrier" photo-etch set
- Bronco 35147 "WW II US Army M3A1 37 mm anti-tank gun" kit

1-2 The kit comes from the Italian company Italeri, reference code 245. It is a veteran kit that comes with all the good and bad things typical of the time in which it was released, so we need to do an extra job of detailing an upgrading.

3 We start by building and painting the cab of the truck. That way, the different components can be painted without other pieces of the model getting in the way.

4 The same process for the seats.

5 Some parts of the kit are ill-defined or out of scale, like the wood of the backseats, so it was decided to build them from scratch. For that, some Evergreen strips were cut, measuring them against the ones in the kit.

6 With a sharp knife, the grain in the strips was simulated, and rivets were added that fasten each wooden strip in place.

7 The same was done with the seats, adding a piece of tinfoil, shaped so it resembled the canvas cover of the seat.

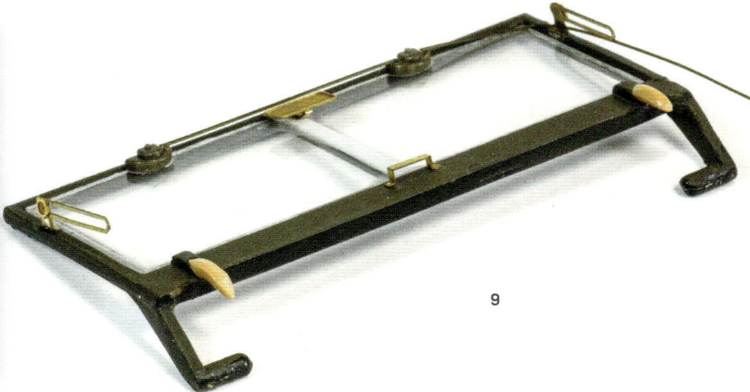

8 The solid lamps were hollowed with a drill and 3 mm lens was inserted.

9 In the windshield, the transparent pieces of the kit were changed for a clear acetate sheet. After that, the sheet was detailed by using the photo-etch set and adding the motor and cable of the windshield wiper.

10 The radiator grill is practically useless, so the Limes one was used, laser-cut in cardboard and with some metallic wire.

11 The 37 mm gun was discarded, using only its shield which had to be thinned down a lot with some sandpaper and patience. In its place, the excellent Bronco gun was used with a scratch-built frame that fixed it to the shield. For building this references of the real thing were used.

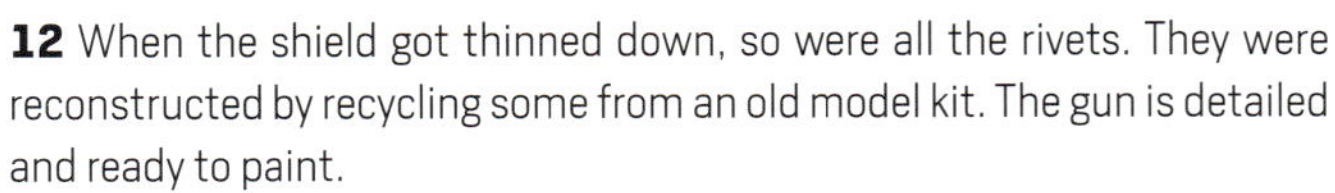

12 When the shield got thinned down, so were all the rivets. They were reconstructed by recycling some from an old model kit. The gun is detailed and ready to paint.

13

14

15

16

13 The front of the vehicle was detailed with the Eduard photo-etch set. The cable of the winch is made of braided wire.

14 The side box of the kit was also replaced by a scratch-built box with plastic and photo-etch spares.

15 The same procedure was used for the gun base, because the base in the kit doesn't match reality. Again, using real-life references will be very helpful.

16 The shovel comes from the always useful bits-box. The straps were detailed with the use of photo-etch spares.

17

17 On the upper part of the bumper, some screws were added which were missing in the original kit.

18 The model is ready to be painted. The gun was painted separately to make things easier.

18

19 The wheels are the original ones of the kit. They come in two halves, so they need to be glued and properly sanded until the joint is invisible.

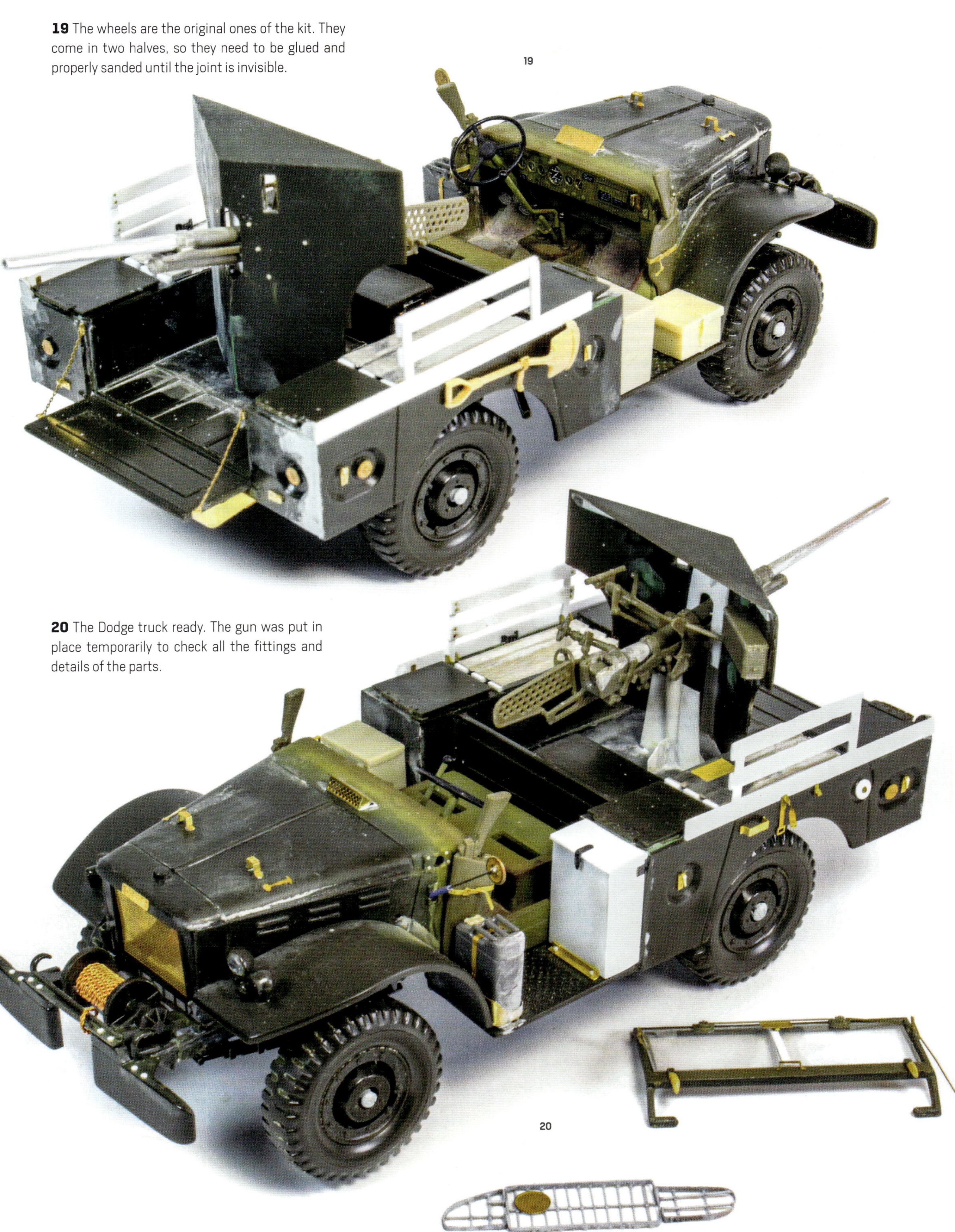
19

20

20 The Dodge truck ready. The gun was put in place temporarily to check all the fittings and details of the parts.

DODGE WC55 37 MM M6 ANTI-TANK

WHEELS

21 The wheels are painted first with a basecoat of Black Primer 73.602.

22 The interior was painted with the omnipresent US Olive Drab 71.043, this time highlighted a bit with some US Light Green 71.137.

23 Dark Rubber 70.306 was dry-brushed over the tires.

24 A really thin wash of Beige 70.917 was applied, so that the paint would be especially noticeable in the joints between tire and rim.

25 Rust effects were applied on the central part of the rim with Hull Red 70.985 and Light Rust Wash 70.505.

26 The pigments Light Slate Grey 73.113 and Light Sienna 73.104 were used, applied dry, to simulate the dirt which adhered to the tire tread.

27 With a small thin brush some radial dirt stain lines were applied with Rain Marks 73.819.

28 The wheels were finished with a bit of Oil Stains 73.813.

29 The vehicle was airbrushed with US Olive Drab 71.043 and highlighted a bit with some US Light Green 71.137. This way, the camouflage application to follow would be slightly less contrasting and the various parts would look better together.

29

30 The filter Desert Dust Wash 76.522 was applied on the horizontal areas.

30

31

31 Another filter was added in the most hidden areas with Sepia Wash 73.200.

DODGE WC55 37 MM M6 ANTI-TANK

32 Now was the time for decals, and with Decal Softener 73.212 and Decal Fix 73.213 the US Army plates and the usual white star were applied.

35

33 For the yellow stars used in Tunisia, a transfer sheet from Archer came in handy.

34 Finally, the decals were protected by airbrushing them with a coat of Permanent Matt Varnish 70.520.

35 The camouflage is replicated with Iraqi Sand 70.819 applied with a brush.

36 The canvas of the seats was painted with a mix of Green Brown 70.879 and Beige 70.917.

RUST STEEL PLATE

37 Next the steel plate, where the base of the gun stands, was painted with a basecoat of Panzer Dark Grey 71.056.

38 Different orange, red and blue tones were applied with a sponge.

39 Next a wash of Dark Rust 76.507 was applied.

40 To simulate the chipping and wear, a coat of Chipping Medium was airbrushed.

40 And over this, the basecoat color was applied.

41 After letting the Chipping Medium dry for 10 to 15 minutes, the base color was removed with a damp brush until the effect looked convincing, the moisture on the brush reacted with the Chipping Medium and removed chips of the top layer of paint to leave a very realistic finish.

42 Some moderate and logical rusted chipping was next applied with Hull Red 70.985.

43 The edges were worked on with a graphite pen and a blending stump.

44 Also, the grain of the wood was simulated with Gold Brown 70.877 and Beige 70.917 on those areas where the paint would have flaked off.

45 Now the wear on the vehicle was simulated with oils, by applying small amounts of white, ochres and yellows.

46 With a brush dampened with white spirit and used in a circular motion, the different tones were blended. An application oil enhances the shades of color in a very effective and subtle way.

47 Some dust was airbrushed on the lower part of the vehicle with Aged White 71.132.

48 Here now is a good foundation for some mud splashes.

49

50

49-50 These splashes are a mix of pigments and sifted plaster.

DODGE WC55 37 MM M6 ANTI-TANK

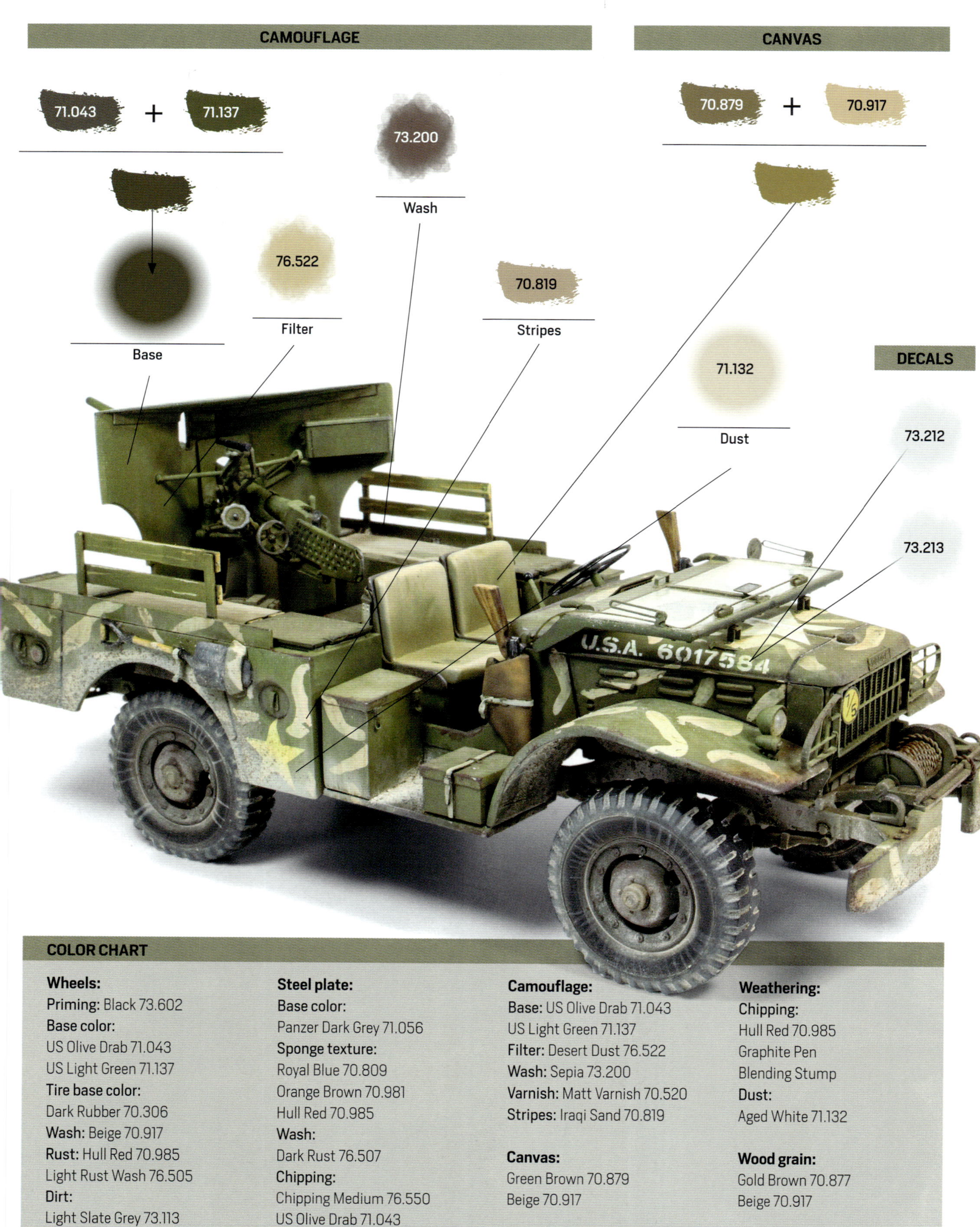

COLOR CHART

Wheels:
Priming: Black 73.602
Base color:
US Olive Drab 71.043
US Light Green 71.137
Tire base color:
Dark Rubber 70.306
Wash: Beige 70.917
Rust: Hull Red 70.985
Light Rust Wash 76.505
Dirt:
Light Slate Grey 73.113
Light Sienna 73.104
Rain Marks 73.819
Oil Stains 73.813

Steel plate:
Base color:
Panzer Dark Grey 71.056
Sponge texture:
Royal Blue 70.809
Orange Brown 70.981
Hull Red 70.985
Wash:
Dark Rust 76.507
Chipping:
Chipping Medium 76.550
US Olive Drab 71.043
US Light Green 71.137

Camouflage:
Base: US Olive Drab 71.043
US Light Green 71.137
Filter: Desert Dust 76.522
Wash: Sepia 73.200
Varnish: Matt Varnish 70.520
Stripes: Iraqi Sand 70.819

Canvas:
Green Brown 70.879
Beige 70.917

Decals:
Decal Softener 73.212
Decal Fix 73.213

Weathering:
Chipping:
Hull Red 70.985
Graphite Pen
Blending Stump
Dust:
Aged White 71.132

Wood grain:
Gold Brown 70.877
Beige 70.917

STEEL PLATE

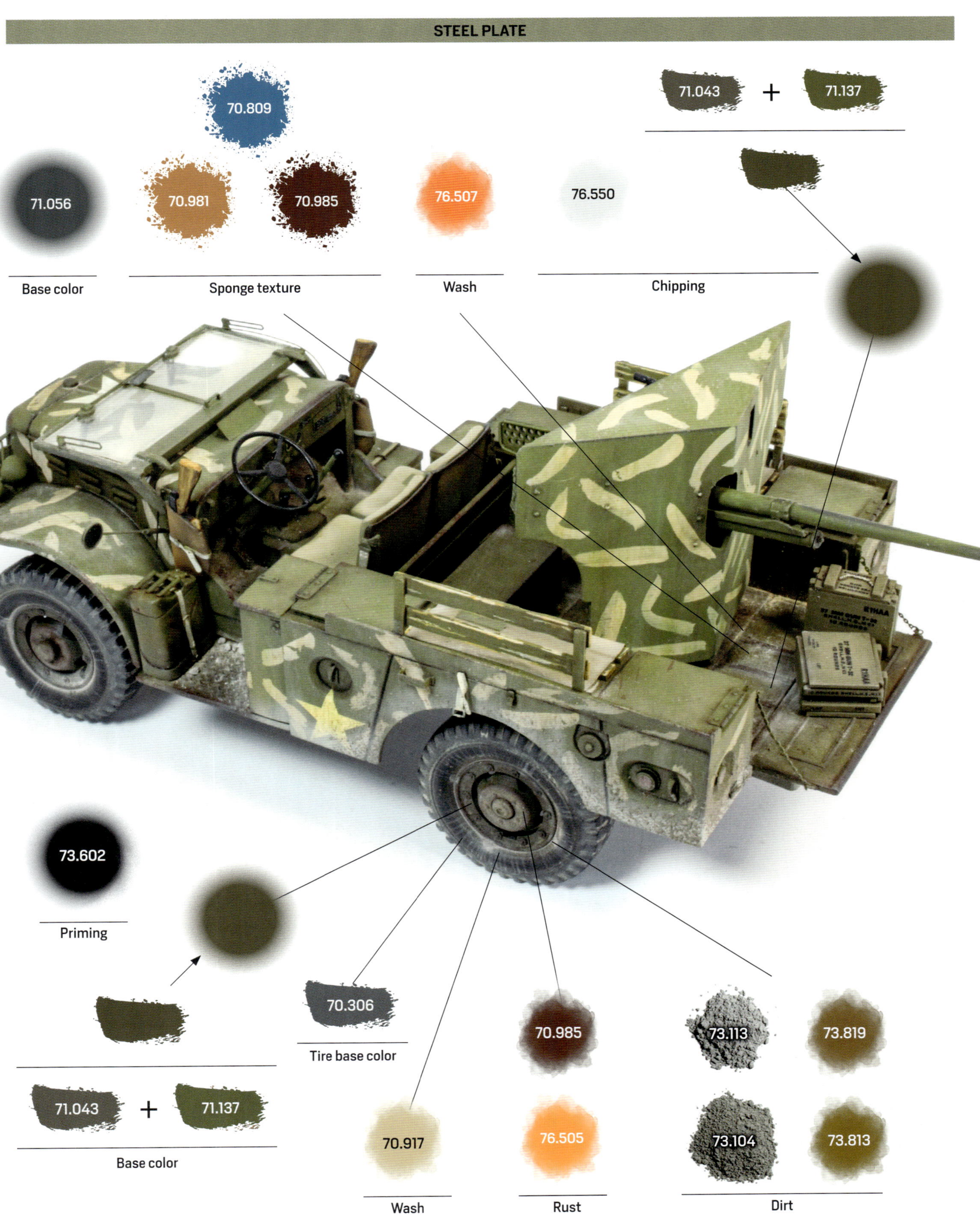

WHEELS

M5A1 STUART

ROI-NAMUR, MARSHALL ISLANDS, 1944

Following the strategy of jumping from Pacific island to island to reach Japan, and once the obstacle of the island of Tarawa had been overcome, the US forces prepared to occupy the Marshall Islands, a group of twenty-nine atolls and five islands. The US landing on these islands would be the first step in the plan to penetrate the "outer rim" of the Japanese defensive perimeter in the Pacific Ocean.

The plan was codenamed "Operation Flintlock" and consisted of Task Force 51 and 52, commanded respectively by Admirals Holland Smith and Richmond K. Turner; the operation would be used to transport an invasion force to the Kwajalein Atoll, while Task Force 53, commanded by Admiral Richard L. Connolly would do the same for the invasion of Roi-Namur. Once those objectives were accomplished, the plan specified that the fleet would sail on to the Eniwetok Atoll. The invasion started on January 31th, 1944, when the American troops landed on a territory that had been in Japanese hands since before Pearl Harbor. The incessant bombardment prior to the landing now inflicted complete devastation across Kwajalein and Roi-Namur.

The defences of Roi-Namur, consisting of bunkers and blockhouses hidden in the dense tropical palm tree jungle, were stronger than expected and had survived the shelling. In the evening, the 23rd Regiment of the 4th Marine Division managed to neutralize some 75 mm artillery positions with flamethrowers and hand grenades but, at the end of the day, progress on both objectives was still slow.

On the second day of the operation, the 4th Marine Division, supported by tanks, managed to completely circle the lagoon in Roi-Namur, eliminating several Japanese positions. On February 3rd, thanks to the "Seabees",

the remaining Japanese defences and bunkers had been blown-up with mines and explosives. The conquest of the island was accomplished on that same day when the Marines captured the central airfield. Roi-Namur had cost the Americans 313 casualties and 502 wounded. All Japanese defenders died in the action.

The relatively easy capture of these islands revealed the amphibious capacity of the US Army and proved that the experience gained in the fierce battle for Tarawa had been put to good use. The Japanese also learned that setting the first line of defence on the beaches was ineffective due to the aero-naval bombardment that always preceded the landings.

The 4th Marine Tank Battalion, a part of the 4th Marine Division, used the light M3A1 tanks during the campaign. These were painted in the regulation color Forest Green No. 11, FS 34079/30F4, a tone slightly blueish and darker than the standard Olive Drab applied by default in the factory on all USMC vehicles. This Forest Green proved to be completely inappropriate for the vehicles landing on the light sand of the beaches and coastal terrain of the Pacific Islands. The crews of these vehicles tried to camouflage them in the field as much as possible, using color No. 3 Sand FS-30277/5C3 and No. 8 Earth Red FS-30117/7E6 sprayed in transverse stripes or applied with a brush.

The vehicles had no white stars or license plates but they were given names, a tradition inherited from the Army, by using the first letter of their company, except for the 4th MTB which didn't use the usual first letters of the alphabet, but the letters H, I, J and K. As a norm, this unit painted the tactical division insignia on all the vehicles, a half-circle with three digits which indicated regiment, battalion and company.

M5A1 STUART

1

1 To portray one of the M5A1 used by the 4th Marine Battalion we have chosen a kit from AFV Club, reference AF35105, which is based on the early model used by that unit.

The kit is very good, with excellent detail, and in building presented no problems worth mentioning.

2

3

2 Starting with the running gear, the wheels were changed for those from the Miniarm resin set which are better detailed in both sides

3 The bogie already built. There are two of them on each side.

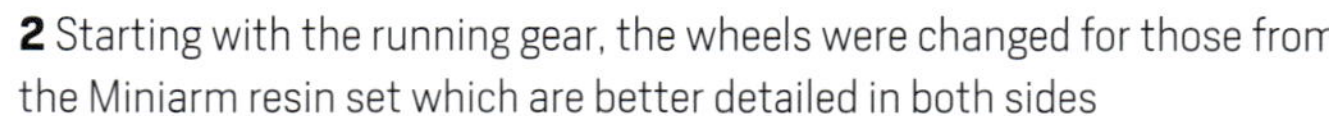

4 The tensioning sprocket was replaced with another one from an old Tamiya kit.

5 The different parts already built and detailed.

4

5

6

7

6 The fording gear was built with photo-etch spares and Evergreen plastic bits.
7 Here is the assembly of the fording system, with the motor chamber of the tank.
8 The machinegun in turned brass adds an excellent detail.
9 The periscopes and headlight covers were much improved when they were replaced with some photo-etched parts.
10 The rear antenna gets detailed with the specific photo-etch part, its resin base and the cable are made with stretched plastic.

8

9

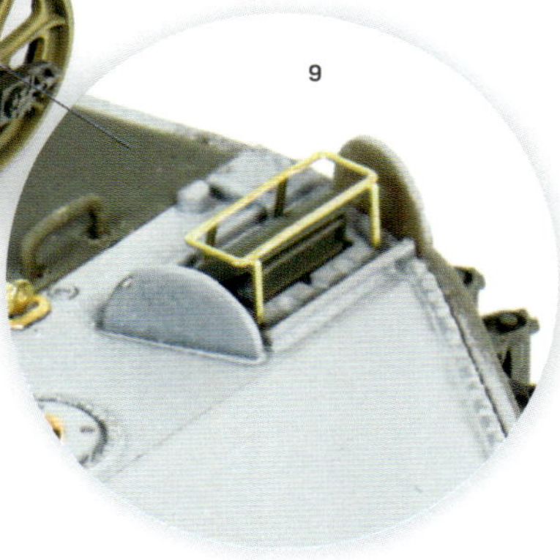

11

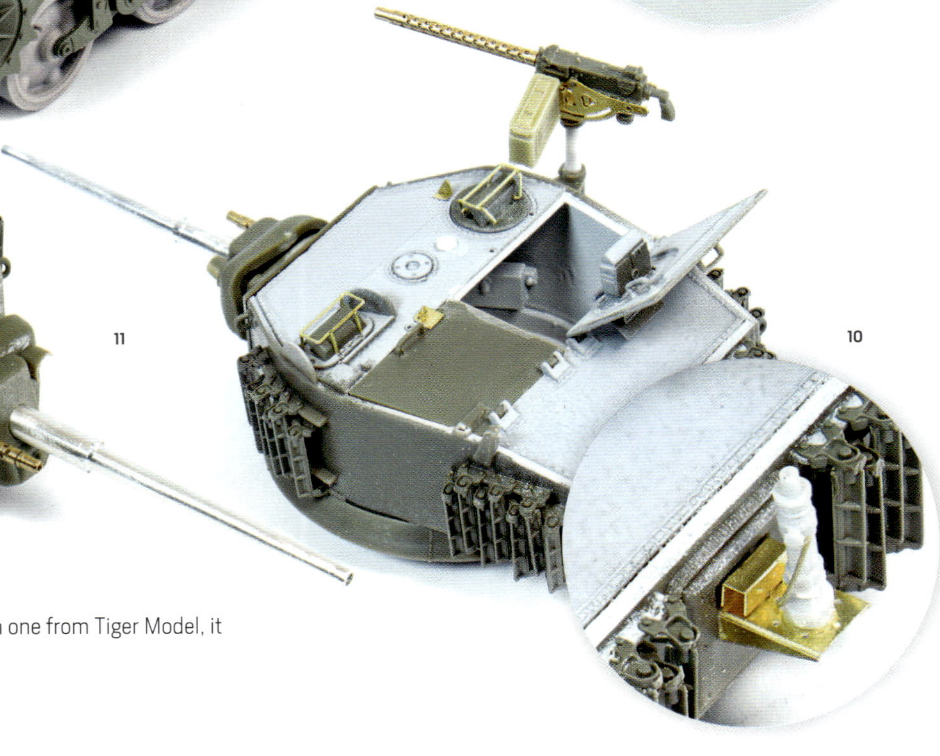

10

11 The upper plate of the turret was replaced with one from Tiger Model, it adapted very easily.

MATERIALS USED

- E.T. Model E35-187 “M5A1 Early version” photo-etch set
- RB Model 35B24 “37 mm M6” kit
- Tiger Model Designs “M5A1 Corrected Turret Roof & Hatches” set
- RB Model 35B082 “7,62 mm Browning M1919” kit
- Miniarm 35172 “US light Tank M5 Pressed Road Wheels” set
- M4 Models 35017 “Bases de Antenas Aliadas” set

12

12 For the tires of the roadwheels Dark Rubber 70.306 was chosen as a basecoat.

13 It is always better to finish the lower part of the vehicles first, avoiding any excessive handling afterwards which might ruin the paintjob. For this particular area, pigments have been used, as well as splashes and damp effects.

14 The lower part of the vehicle finished. Now the bogies can be added without having any problems to access the lower areas of the hull.

13

14

15

16

15 As mentioned above, US Forest Green 71.294 is used for the basecoat since it is the standard color of the USMC.

16 The panels are highlighted adding a mix of Ivory 71.075 and Khaki Brown 71.024, to the base color.

19

17 The darker camouflage tone US Earth Red 71.293 is added first, applied with an airbrush in thin coats until the surface is correctly covered.

18 Next Camouflage Sandbeige RAL 1039 71.244 is applied in the same way.

19 The name of the tank is added by using letter decals. In this case, the name is "Hobo", as a reference to the itinerant workers who travelled around the US during the Great Depression.

20 The divisional half-circumference came from the decals sheet for the M5A1 from Bison Decals.

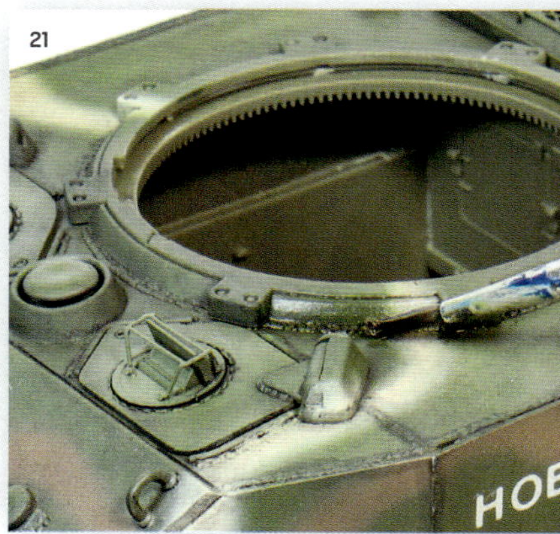

21 The details were outlined with Wash Oiled Earth 76.521, removing any excess if necessary, with a brush dampened in Airbrush Thinner 71.361.

22 Once the washes have dried it can be seen that the colors now look more worn and faded.

23-24 Some chipping was added in a few areas using Hull Red 70.985.

25 The effect of polished metal was obtained with a graphite bar and a blending stump.

26 For the dust effect, UK Light Stone 71.143 was airbrushed, really thinned.

M5A1 STUART

WATER EFFECTS

27 The water stains, typical of the sides of the tank, are made with a fine brush and Rain Marks 73.819 from Weathering Effects.

28 Here Wet Effects 73.828, was applied by airbrush to show moisture, caused by the accumulation of water in the horizontal areas.

29 The result was quite realistic and added more visual effects to the model.

30 This was the moment for working on the accumulation of splashes of mud. For these effects, pigments were mixed with plaster.

31 Water was added to the mixture in order to get a manageable consistency which would flow properly.

32 With a hard bristle brush and a toothpick, spatters were applied in the appropriate areas.

33 Any spatters which landed on an area which was unlikely to be affected were removed with a brush moistened with water. It was important to realize that once the mix had dried, its shade would be much lighter.

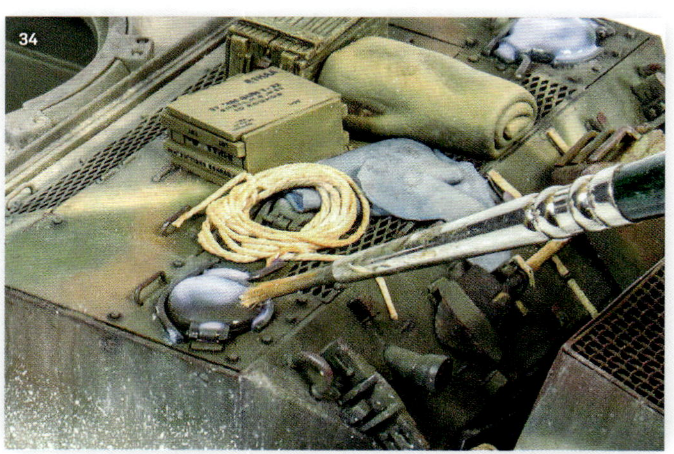

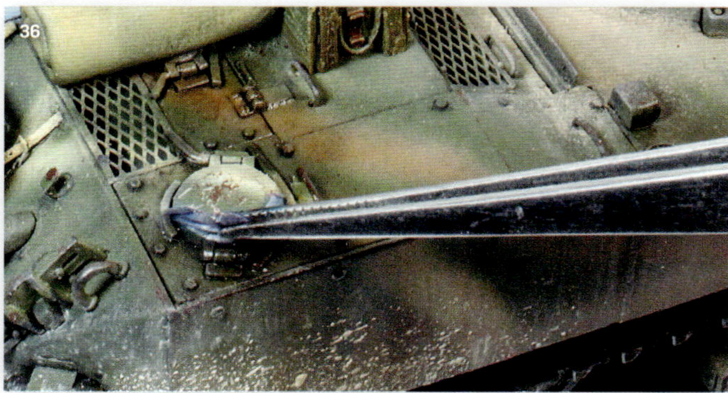

34 Next were the oil spills. The lids of the deposits were protected with Liquid Mask 70.523.

35 Oil Stains 73.813 was airbrushed over the lids.

36 Once the oil stains had dried, the Liquid Mask was carefully removed.

37 In the central parts, Fuel Stains 73.814 was applied with a brush.

38 Once the leftovers of the previous mix used for the mud spatters were dry, they were squashed to obtain small clods of dry dirt.

39 These small clods of dry dirt were applied over the horizontal surface of the running gear, where mud and dry earth would have accumulated in a natural way. Finally, the clods were fixed by applying Pigment Binder 26.233 through capillary action with the help of a brush.

M5A1 STUART

WEATHERING

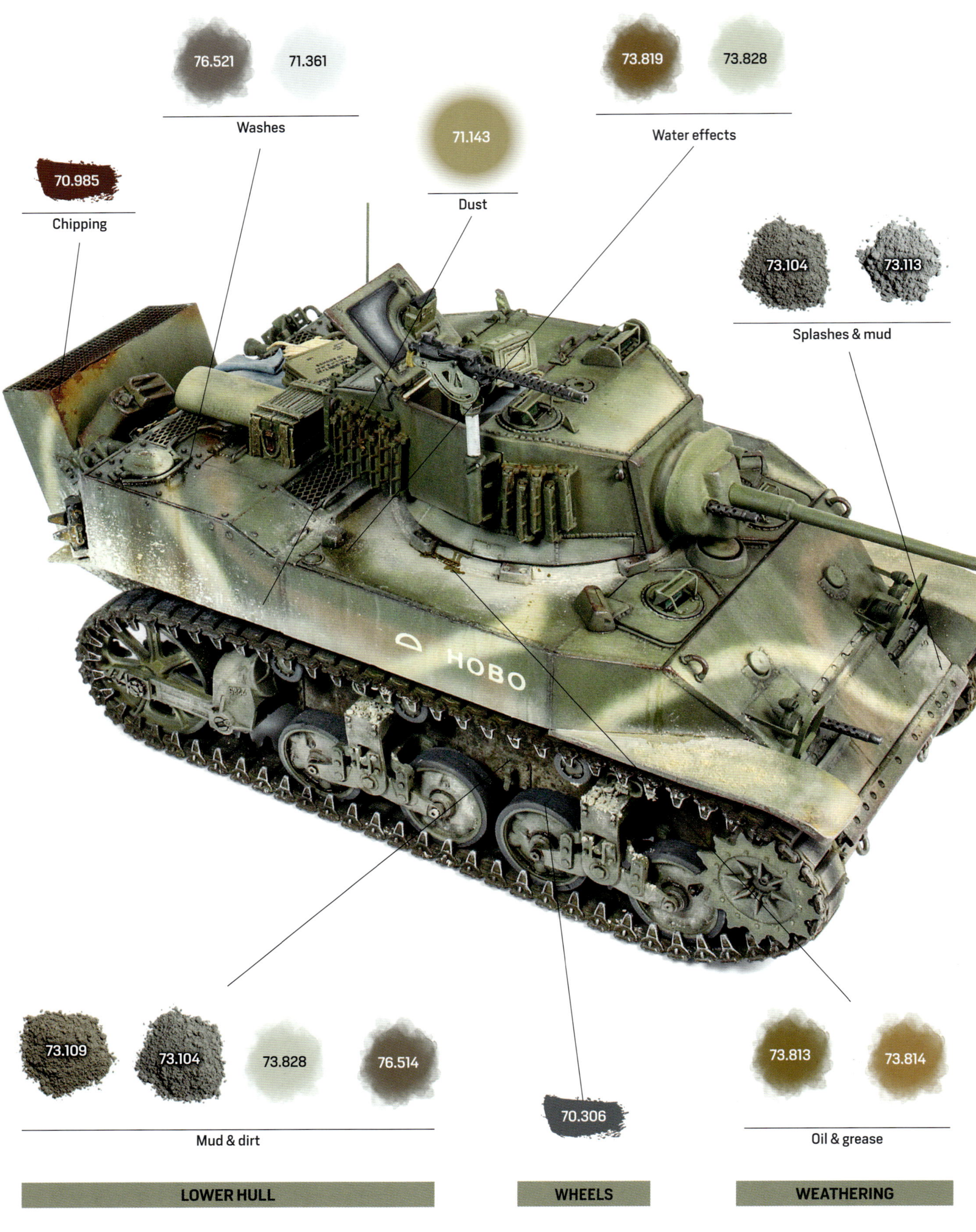

CAMOUFLAGE

COLOR CHART

Wheels:
Dark Rubber 70.306

Lower hull:
Mud & dirt:
Natural Umber 73.109
Light Sienna 73.104
Wet Effects 73.828
Dark Brown 76.514
Rain Marks 73.819

Camouflage:
Base color:
US Forest Green 71.294
Highlights:
Ivory 71.075
Khaki Brown 71.024
Brown color:
US Earth Red 71.293
Sand color:
Sand Beige 71.244

Weathering:
Washes:
Oiled Earth 76.521
Airbrush Thinner 71.361
Chipping:
Hull Red 70.985
Graphite Bar
Dust:
UK Light Stone 71.143
Water effects:
Rain Marks 73.819
Wet Effects 73.828
Splashes & mud:
Light Sienna 73.104
Light Skate Grey 73.113
Plaster
Oil & grease:
Oil Stains 73.813
Fuel Stains 73.814

Pigment Binder 26.233

LVT(A)-2

SAIPAN, MARIANA ISLANDS, 1944

After the US Navy had conquered the Gilbert and Marshall Islands, the Mariana Islands were the next objective: they included Saipan in the north, Tinian in the centre and Guam in the south. Of these islands, the US Navy chose to land first on Saipan, mostly because the Japanese had already built three airfields on that island.

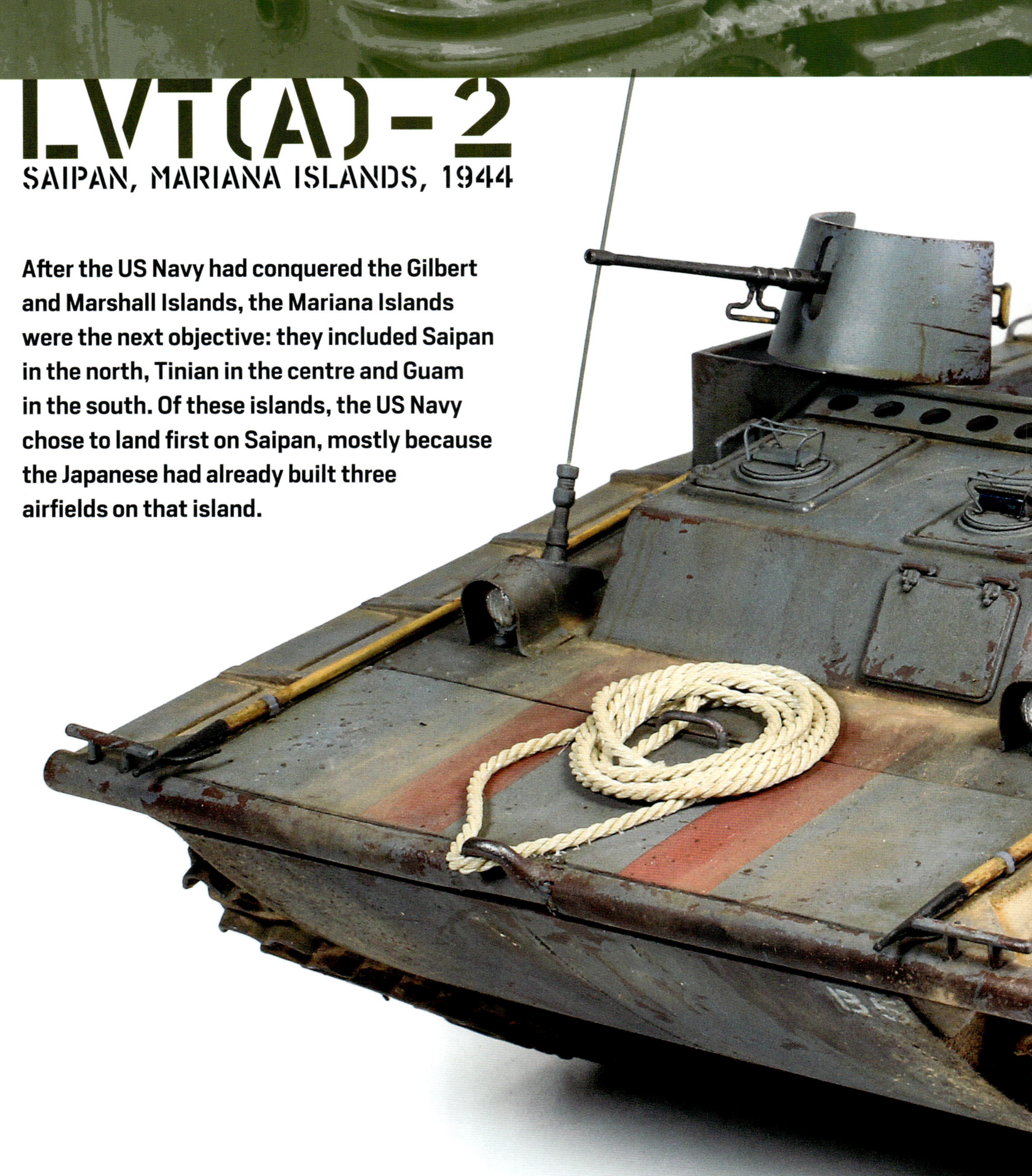

On June 15th 1944, at 07:00 a.m., the invasion started as the 2nd and 4th Marine Divisions, along with more than 700 Amtraks from Admiral Spruance's task force, landed on the beaches of Saipan. Meanwhile, the 27th US Army Infantry Division, still on board the ships, was kept in reserve. The previous day, fifteen Navy battleships had prepared the terrain with a fierce bombing of the island.

Under heavy Japanese fire, the Marines managed to break through and consolidate an extensive beachhead at the end of the day. The following day, the 27th US Army Infantry Division had landed and was occupying the Aslito airfield.

After the defeat of Admiral Ozawa in the Battle of the Philippine Sea, the Japanese garrison, without hope of further help, kept resisting and fighting ferociously. Finally, on July 9th, 1944, at 16:15, the operation commander, Admiral Richmond Turner, officially announced the conquest of Saipan.

The Imperial Japanese Army suffered more than 29000 casualties and the defence of the Mariana Islands was seriously compromised. The disaster was of such magnitude that Vice-Admiral Nagumo committed suicide. The defeat in the Philippine Sea and the fall of Saipan also had another very important political consequence, the resignation of Prime Minister Tojo and his government.

The Amtrack used by the 2nd Armored Amphibian Battalion in the landings on the designated beaches in the north of Saipan were painted in No. 14 Ocean Grey – FS35164, according to Navy regulations. They neither had white stars nor any other insignia excepting the number and company and the invasion stripes on the side and prowl of the vehicle. In addition, the vehicles had one and two red stripes for Red Beach 1 and 2, and one or two green stripes for Green Beach 1 and 2.

LVT(A)-2

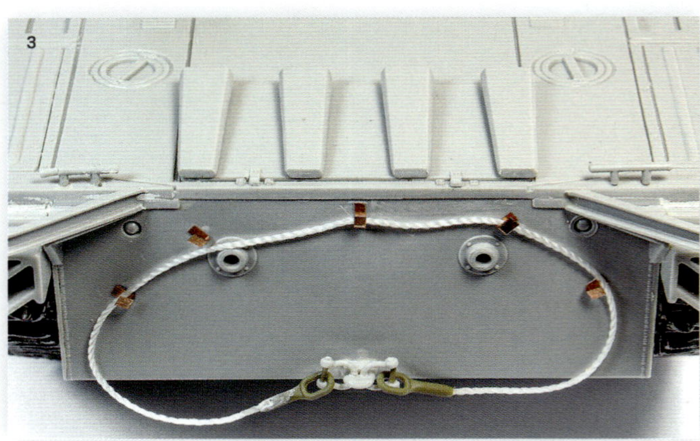

1 The model kit is made by Italeri, reference 6470. This time, the kit is built just out of the box, with only some small custom improvements. Building the model is easy and does not present any particular problems. It is a simple kit with good fit, as is usual with Italeri. The tracks are the only problem worth mentioning, these are made with an excessively rigid vinyl and with just two portions for each set, which complicates the tiresome work of joining them together.

2 In the back of the barge, a Browning machinegun was added from another kit.

3 Brackets were added for the towing cable with copper foil and the cable itself was made with net repair thread.

4 On the front, the headlamps and their covers, which came in one piece, were replaced with some headlamps from the bits box, with some lenses added. For the covers copper foil was used. The periscopes of the hatches came from Verlinden and the spare covers from a photo-etch set for the Sherman tank.

5 This time the tracks had to be glued with cyanoacrylate before painting them.

7

6

8

6 The ropes were also made with net repair thread.

7-8 The finished model, ready to start the painting process.

CHIPPING

9 For a start the whole kit was airbrushed with RAL8012 Surface Primer Ger. Red Brown 73.605

10 The first filter was applied over the surface, using Light Rust 71.130 to break down the base color.

11 Once dry, a second filter was applied, this time with Red Wash 73.206.

12 The previous work was protected with a coat of Polyurethane Gloss Varnish 26.650, applied thinly with the airbrush.

13 Next, a coat of Chipping Medium 76.550 was airbrushed on the surface, and over it, the color Ocean Grey 71.273 was applied.

14 Some color contrast was added on some panels and areas with blue and grey tones, applied in the same way as the basecoat.

15 With a damp brush and a toothpick, chipping was started in a random way, insisting more in the most logical areas.

16 More subtle effects were added, using a sponge and a reddish-brown tone, Surface Primer Ger. Red Brown 73.605.

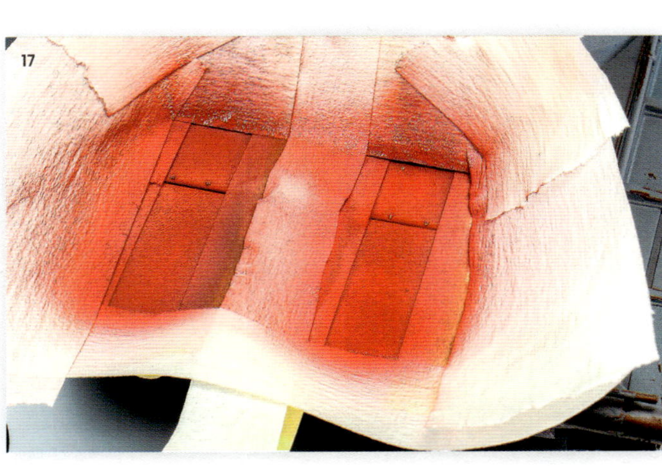

17 After protecting the previous work with a new coat of varnish, a template was prepared and painted with Red RLM23 71.003.

18 For the red side stripes, the decals that came with the kit were used, cutting to shape before applying them with Decal Fix 73.213 and Decal Softener 73.212. The same was done with the number which came from another extra decal sheet.

19 The barge interior received a first weathering with dry pigments that were set on the surface with Pigment Binder 26.233.

20 Small areas were worked on in succession, dampening first with White Spirit and applying small portions of color that were blended with a flat brush in delicate vertical strokes.

21 Once the colors had dried, the grey tone looked appropriately dull and discoloured.

22 Water splashes were added on the side planks, airbrushing with Wet Effects 73.828.

23 With some Rain Marks 73.819 applied with a brush, a more intense contrast was added to the water spilling in some areas.

24 Using a brush and a toothpick, spatters of dirt, water and mud were applied with the Washes Pale Grey 73.202 and Sepia 73.200 and also with Flat Flesh 70.955.

25 Diverse equipment was added and set in place with vinyl glue.

26 The machine guns were painted with Black 71.057, and afterwards the metallic surfaces were polished with graphite powder, applied with the finger.

27 The oil stains were brushed on with Engine Grime 73.815.

28 Some water puddles were added inside the barge with Rain Marks 73.819.

29 A pair of pin-up posters added the "human touch".

30 Rust was added to the track covers by airbrushing with Light Rust Wash 76.505.

31 The ropes were dampened with vinyl glue and water, shaped in the desired form, and allowed to dry.

32 The half-burnt oil residues of the exhaust pipes were achieved with Fuel Stains 73.814.

33 Dirt and mud residues, due to the action of the tracks, were placed on the horizontal planes and set in place with Pigment Binder 26.233.

B5
B5

CAMOUFLAGE

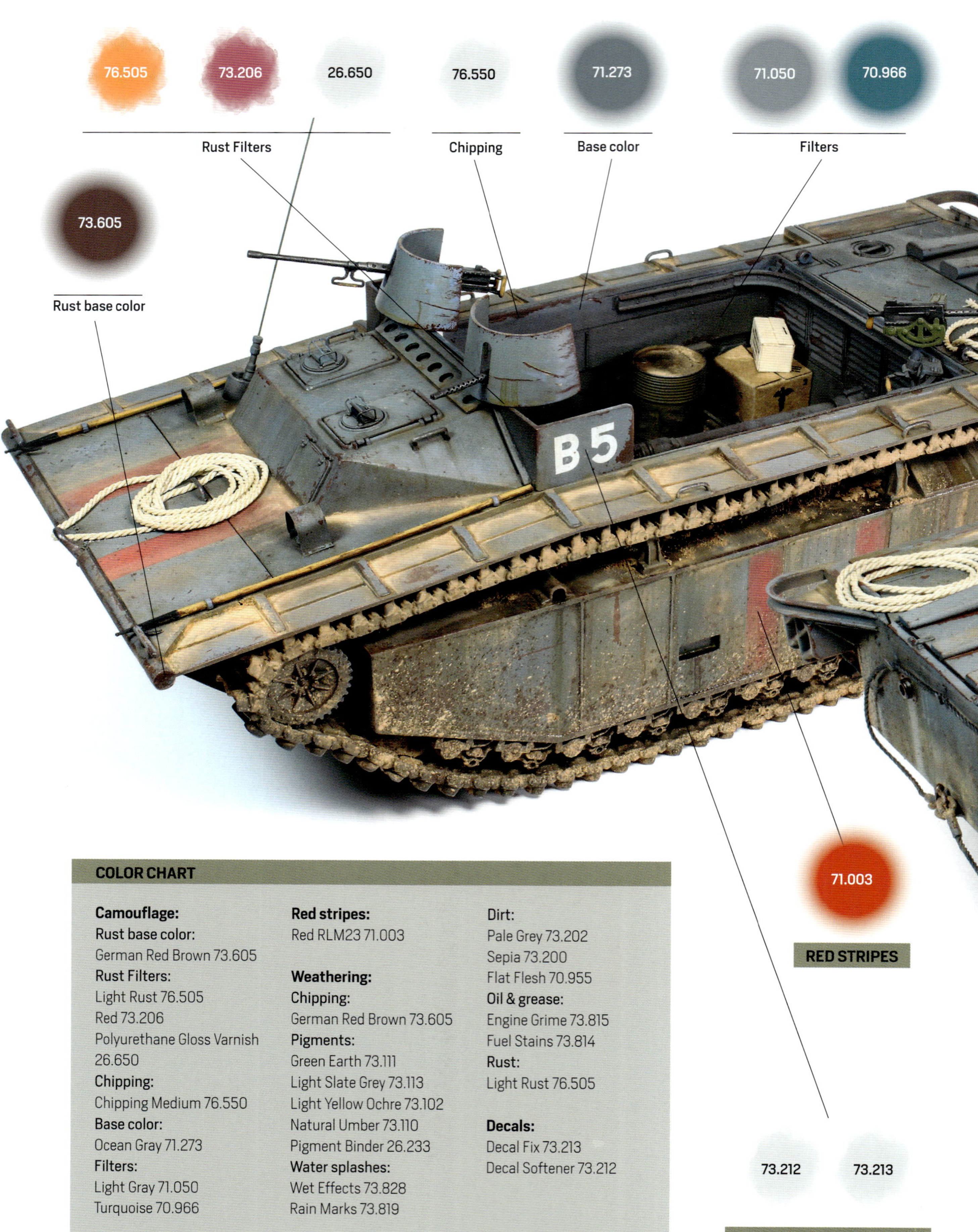

COLOR CHART

Camouflage:
Rust base color:
German Red Brown 73.605
Rust Filters:
Light Rust 76.505
Red 73.206
Polyurethane Gloss Varnish 26.650
Chipping:
Chipping Medium 76.550
Base color:
Ocean Gray 71.273
Filters:
Light Gray 71.050
Turquoise 70.966

Red stripes:
Red RLM23 71.003

Weathering:
Chipping:
German Red Brown 73.605
Pigments:
Green Earth 73.111
Light Slate Grey 73.113
Light Yellow Ochre 73.102
Natural Umber 73.110
Pigment Binder 26.233
Water splashes:
Wet Effects 73.828
Rain Marks 73.819

Dirt:
Pale Grey 73.202
Sepia 73.200
Flat Flesh 70.955
Oil & grease:
Engine Grime 73.815
Fuel Stains 73.814
Rust:
Light Rust 76.505

Decals:
Decal Fix 73.213
Decal Softener 73.212

WEATHERING

73.605
Chipping
73.111
73.113
73.102
73.110
26.233
Pigments
B5
73.815
73.814
Oil & grease
73.828
73.819
Water splashes
73.202
73.200
73.955
Dirt
76.505
Rust

SHERMAN M4A1

AACHEN, AUTUMN 1944

American armour was unable to cross the rubble-blocked streets and it was suicidal for the infantry to try moving into the city ruins which were full of snipers. Finally, the infantry had to resort to the 155mm guns of the M12 self-propelled artillery, which knocked down all the buildings defended by the Germans and destroyed one by one all their fortified bastions. It was one of the biggest urban battles fought by American forces in World War Two.

At last, on October 21th, 1944, the remnants of the German garrison surrendered. Aachen was the first German city captured by the Allies in the war. It was also the point where the Western defensive wall - designated the" Siegfried Line"- was broken.

The conquest of Aachen would not have meant much more to the Allies than that of any other city, but its effect on the morale of the German population was tremendous. The defeat proved the vulnerability of the Siegfried Line, it showed that the Allied Forces had recovered quickly after the setback of Operation Market Garden and had now gained a foothold on German soil.

Since June 1944, after the D Day landings in Normandy, the advancing Allied Forces had inflicted defeat after defeat on the formerly invincible German Army, now forced to retreat to the very frontiers of the 'Thousand-Year Reich'. In September 1944, the Allies began the maneuvers to circle the city of Aachen on the furthest southern border of Germany; these maneuvers were completed on October 16th by the VII Corps of the US Army, commanded by General J. L. Collins. The actual offensive for the conquest of the city started on the 13th of October. The German defenders under the command of General Hermann Balck, resisted tenaciously during a full week of fierce street fighting, under conditions favorable to the Germans who knew the terrain well.

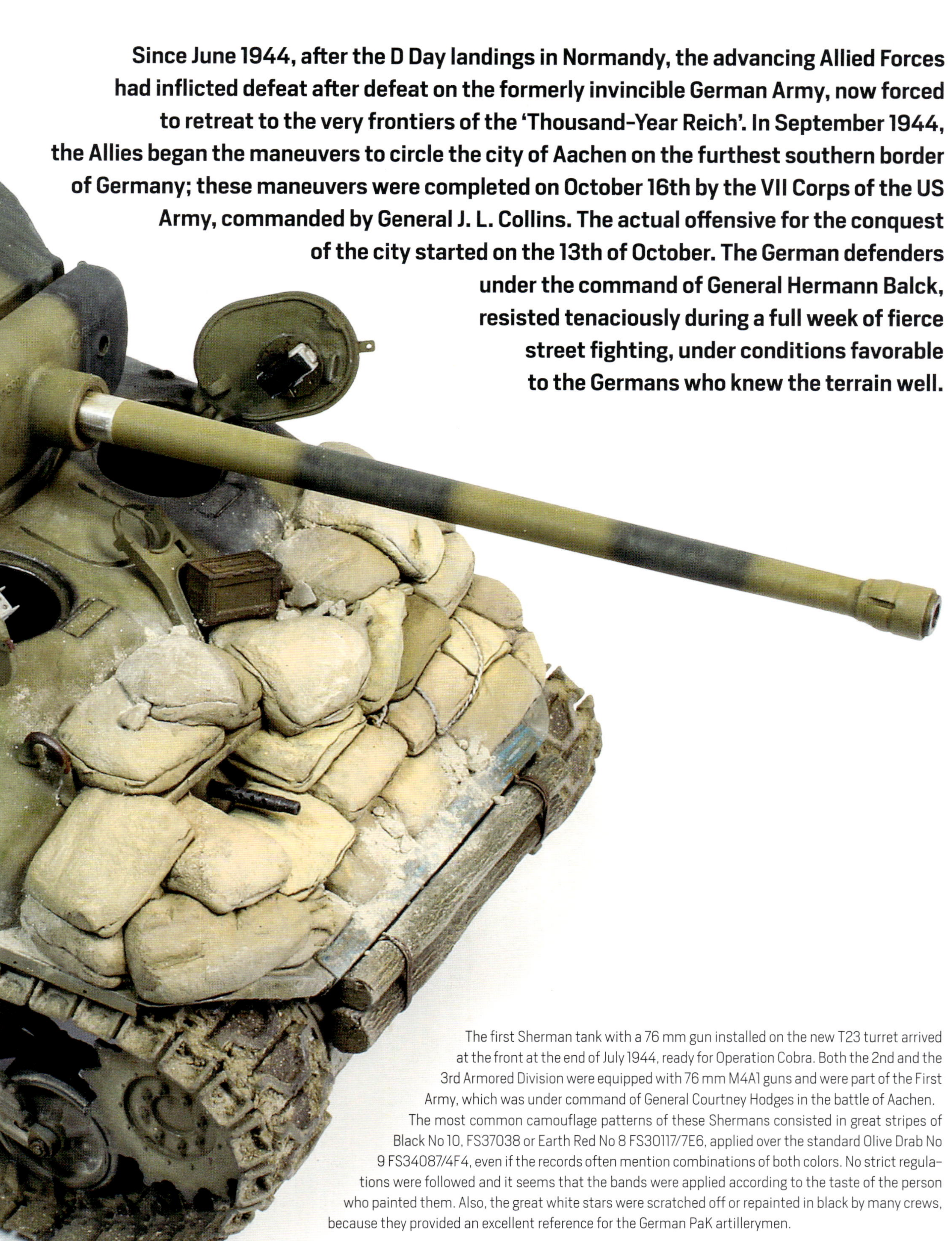

The first Sherman tank with a 76 mm gun installed on the new T23 turret arrived at the front at the end of July 1944, ready for Operation Cobra. Both the 2nd and the 3rd Armored Division were equipped with 76 mm M4A1 guns and were part of the First Army, which was under command of General Courtney Hodges in the battle of Aachen. The most common camouflage patterns of these Shermans consisted in great stripes of Black No 10, FS37038 or Earth Red No 8 FS30117/7E6, applied over the standard Olive Drab No 9 FS34087/4F4, even if the records often mention combinations of both colors. No strict regulations were followed and it seems that the bands were applied according to the taste of the person who painted them. Also, the great white stars were scratched off or repainted in black by many crews, because they provided an excellent reference for the German PaK artillerymen.

1

MATERIALS USED

- Aber 35032 "Sherman M4, M4A1, M4A3" photo-etch set
- Value Gear SB008 "Sandbag Fronts for M4A1 Dragon 6083"
- Lion Marc LM60005 "Sherman Brass Skids" set
- MR Models 35521 "Gun barrel 76 mm M1 w. muzzle thread protector for Sherman" set
- Archer 88007 Resin Casting Marks
- RB Model 35B082 "7,62 mm Browning M1919" kit

1 Dragon's M4A1 (76) W "Operation Cobra", reference 6083, is a very good portrayal of the legendary American vehicle. While building this vehicle, it is important to follow the instruction sheet carefully, because there are many extra pieces which can be used to portray other versions of the tank and which can also be very helpful to improve other kits in the future.

2 The gaps for the tools were filled with some plastic bits.

3 Once dry, the surface was levelled with the help of a Dremel tool and a drill.

4 Using the Archer set, the marks were added, as well as the casting numbers which were missing in the turret.

5 The kit's track skids were replaced with some photo-etched parts.

2

3

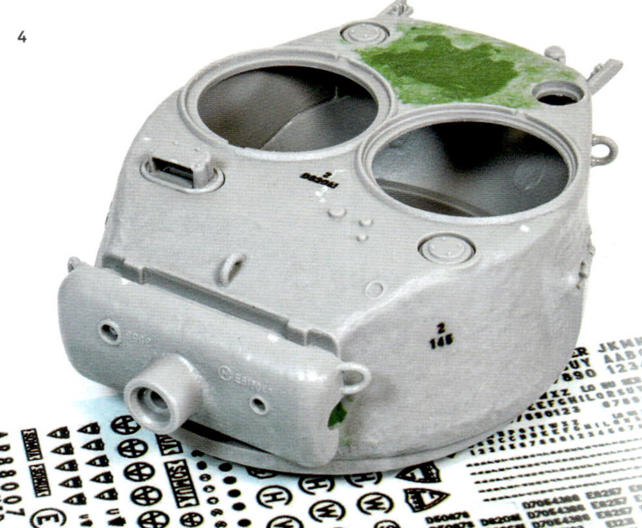

4

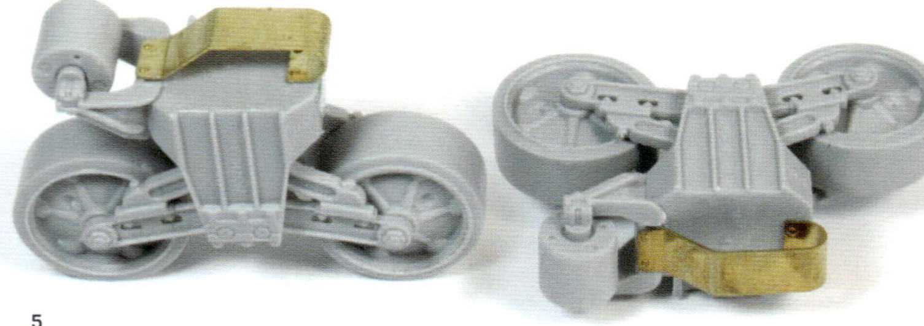

5

6 In the front, the extra sandbags were added from Value Gear, a perfect fit on the kit.

6

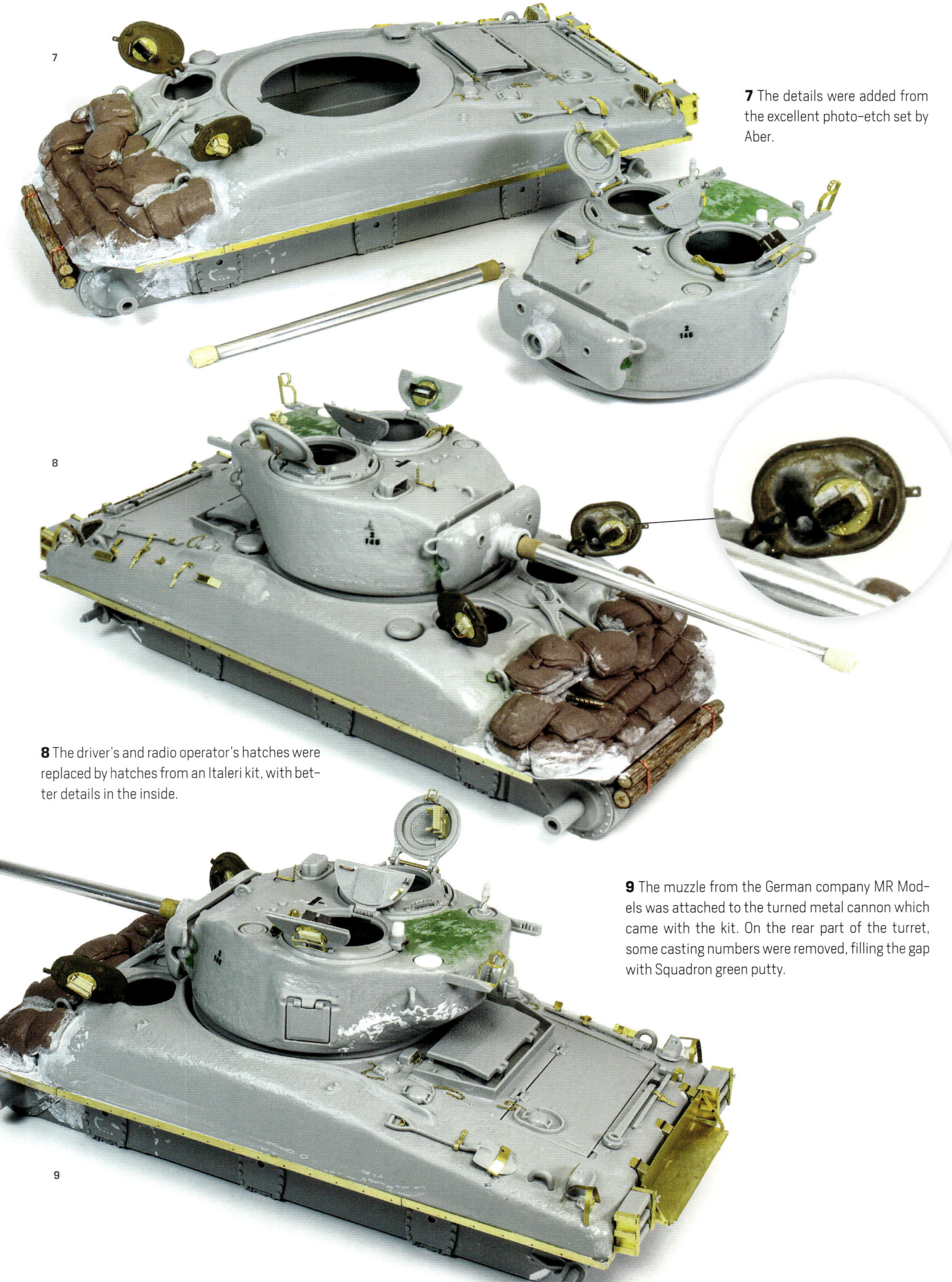

7

7 The details were added from the excellent photo-etch set by Aber.

8

8 The driver's and radio operator's hatches were replaced by hatches from an Italeri kit, with better details in the inside.

9

9 The muzzle from the German company MR Models was attached to the turned metal cannon which came with the kit. On the rear part of the turret, some casting numbers were removed, filling the gap with Squadron green putty.

10

10 Grey Surface Primer 73.601 was airbrushed first.

11 Next a basecoat with US Olive Drab 71.043 was applied.

12 Highlights were applied area by area using an airbrush and Beige 71.074. Next a filter with Desert Dust 76.522 was applied.

13 At this point, the camouflage pattern to be replicated was outlined with a water color pencil.

14 The selected areas were painted with Black 71.057, applied with an airbrush.

11

12

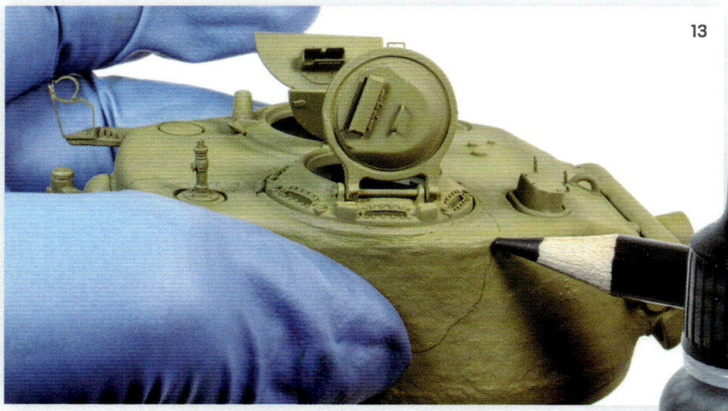

13

14

15

15 The tone was highlighted with Panzer Dark Grey 71.056.

TRACKS

16 Starting with the tracks, a basecoat of Camouflage Sandbeige RAL 1039 71.244 was applied.

17 The pigments Light Sienna 73.104 and Light Slate Grey 73.113 were applied over the surface of the tracks, ensuring their proper penetration in the pattern of the links.

18 A coat of Oiled Earth 76.521 was brushed on the central part.

19 Spatters were applied with different shades of brown from Model Color: Chocolate Brown 70.872, Buff 70.976 and Smoke 70.939.

20

20 Finally some graphite was applied over the pattern and teeth of the links.

21

21 The tracks were added, adjusting and glueing them to a fixed position to finish the initial process of painting.

DECALS

22 A coat of Permanent Gloss Varnish 70.510 was applied in the area of the decals.

23 With the products designed for that task, Decal Softener 73.212 and Decal Fix 73.213, each decal was placed in the right area.

24 A coat of Permanent Matt Varnish 70.520 integrated and protected the decals from the weathering work to come next.

25 Sandbags were painted in ochre and yellow tones, to differentiate and individualize each one of them.

26 Subtle drybrushing was applied over the surface and the details with Sand Yellow 71.028 in the green areas and US Sand 71.138 in the areas painted in black.

27 To simulate overall wear, small amounts of the usual oils were brushed on.

28 Working area by area, different tonalities of color were created by blending the oils with a circular motion of the brush.

29 In the vertical areas, the blending motion was vertical, from up to down.

30 In order to obtain contrast in some parts, green oil paint was applied directly, without dampening the brush in white spirit.

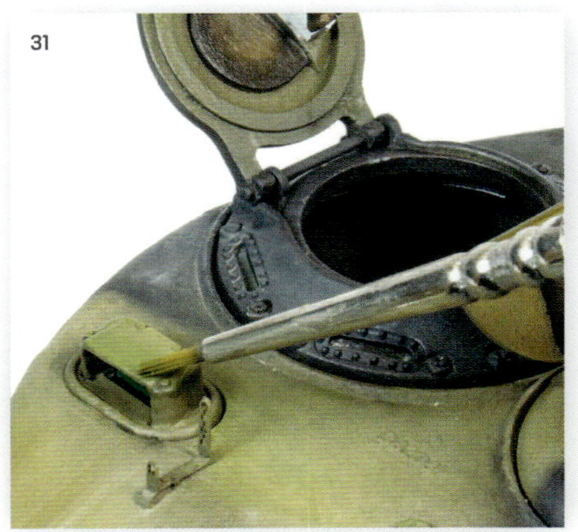

31 More greyish tones were used in the black areas.

32 The most interesting details were enhanced.

33 The stowage on the tank, painted separately, were now incorporated.

34 The tools were painted with a brush, simu-latingsome chipping of the paint.

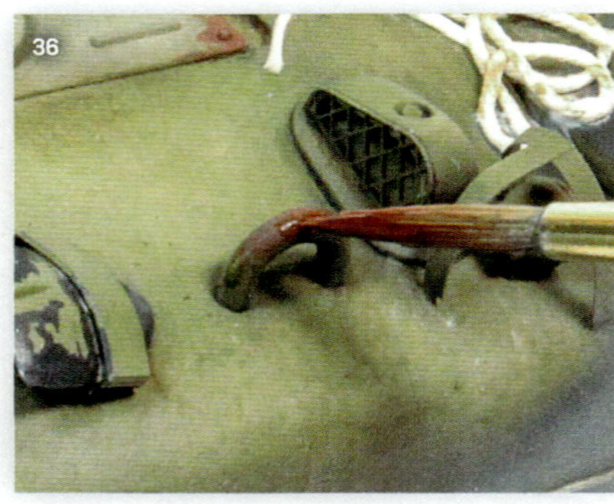

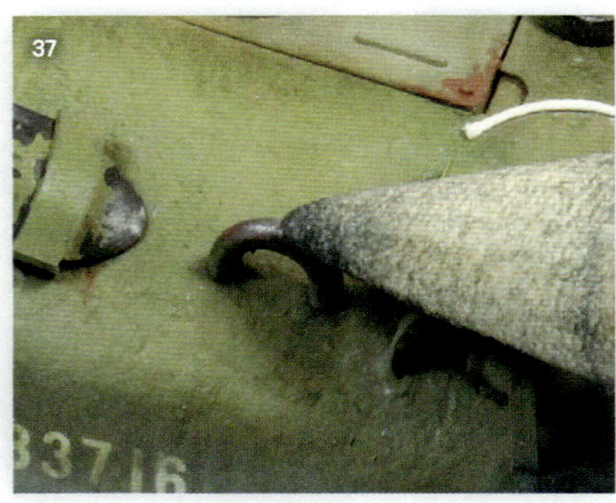

35 Using the sponge technique, some careful chipping was applied in green, US Olive Drab 71.043, over the black painted surfaces.

36 The same was done in the green areas, this time with the color Hull Red 70.985.

37 The metallic effects were achieved with graphite and a blending stump.

38 The spilt oil was painted with Oil Stains 73.813 from the Weathering Effects range.

39 The spilt fuel was airbrushed with Fuel Stains 73.814 also from Weathering Effects.

40 The damp effects were achieved by applying Wet Effects 73.828 with a brush.

41 Adding some footprints left by some of the crew was the final detail, water was used to dampen a stamp made by Calibre 35, which replicates the print of a pair of boots. Some pigment was placed on the stamp.

42 And the stamp was used to place the footprints in the chosen area.

43 If any of the prints are not convincing once dry, they can be easily removed with a water-dampened brush

SHERMAN M4A1

WEATHERING

COLOR CHART

Camouflage:
Priming:
Grey 73.601
Base color:
US Olive Drab 71.043
Highlights:
Beige 71.074
Desert Dust 76.522
Camouflage base color:
Black 71.057
Camouflage highlights:
Panzer Dark Grey 71.056

Tracks:
Base:
Sand Beige 71.244
Pigments:
Light Sienna 73.104
Light Slate Grey 73.113
Wash: Oiled Earth 76.521
Splahes:
Chocolate Brown 70.872
Buff 70.976
Smoke 70.939
Metal: Graphite Bar

Decals:
Gloss Varnish 70.510
Decal Softener 73.212
Decal Fix 73.213
Matt Varnish 70.520

Weathering:
Drybrush:
Sand Yellow 71.028
US Sand 71.138

Chipping:
US Olive Drab 71.043
Hull Red 70.985
Oil & grease:
Oil Stains 73.813
Fuel Stains 73.814
Water effects:
Wet Effects 73.828

CAMOUFLAGE

TRACKS

ARMORED JEEP

BATTLE OF THE BULGE, 1944

Although a series of defeats from Normandy to Belgium had left Germany with little more than the shattered remnants of their army, they made the impossible a reality in December 1944. Hitler reorganized these troops to create a new Army Group and used them not only to defend the Reich from the upcoming Allied assault but to unleash an offensive almost identical to the one that had taken the Allies by surprise in 1940.

With utmost secrecy, Hitler started the arrangements of his last and most desperate gamble, initially codenamed Operation "Wacht am Rhein" (Watch on the Rhine) to mislead Allied intelligence by hinting towards a defensive operation. The code name was changed to "Herbstnebel" (Autumn Mist) a few days before the attack. The offensive that would be the swan song of the Third Reich in the West started at dawn of December 16,1944, during one of the coldest winters in memory,

Once past the initial surprise and after suffering considerable losses, the Americans moved to the offensive, launching the 1st and 3rd US Armies against the attack of the German forces, and managed with great effort to force the enemy on the retreat. On January 28th, the German salient had disappeared. The Battle of the Bulge was over and Germany had lost irreplaceable troops and material.

Several camouflages were applied during this winter of 1944-45, camouflages aimed to cover the OD color that stood out noticeably from the snowy white winter background. According to regulations, all white-washed vehicles needed to keep some thin bands of the original green olive color, in order to break their silhouettes in the forest areas, but most of the units left them out and simply covered the whole vehicle in white. The quality of the paint was poor and prone to degrade and flake off easily, showing again the underlying original olive green color.

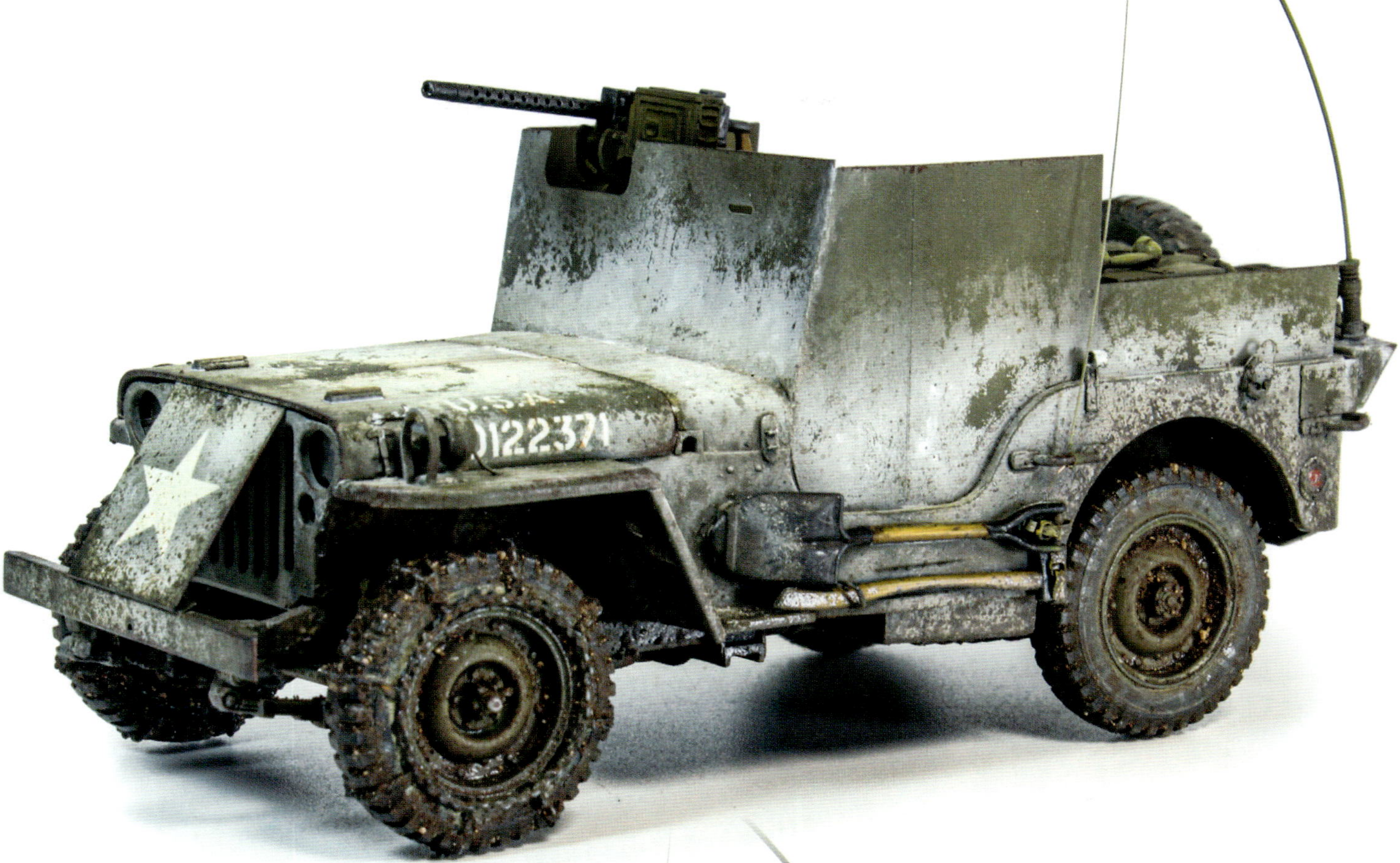
U.S.A.
20122371

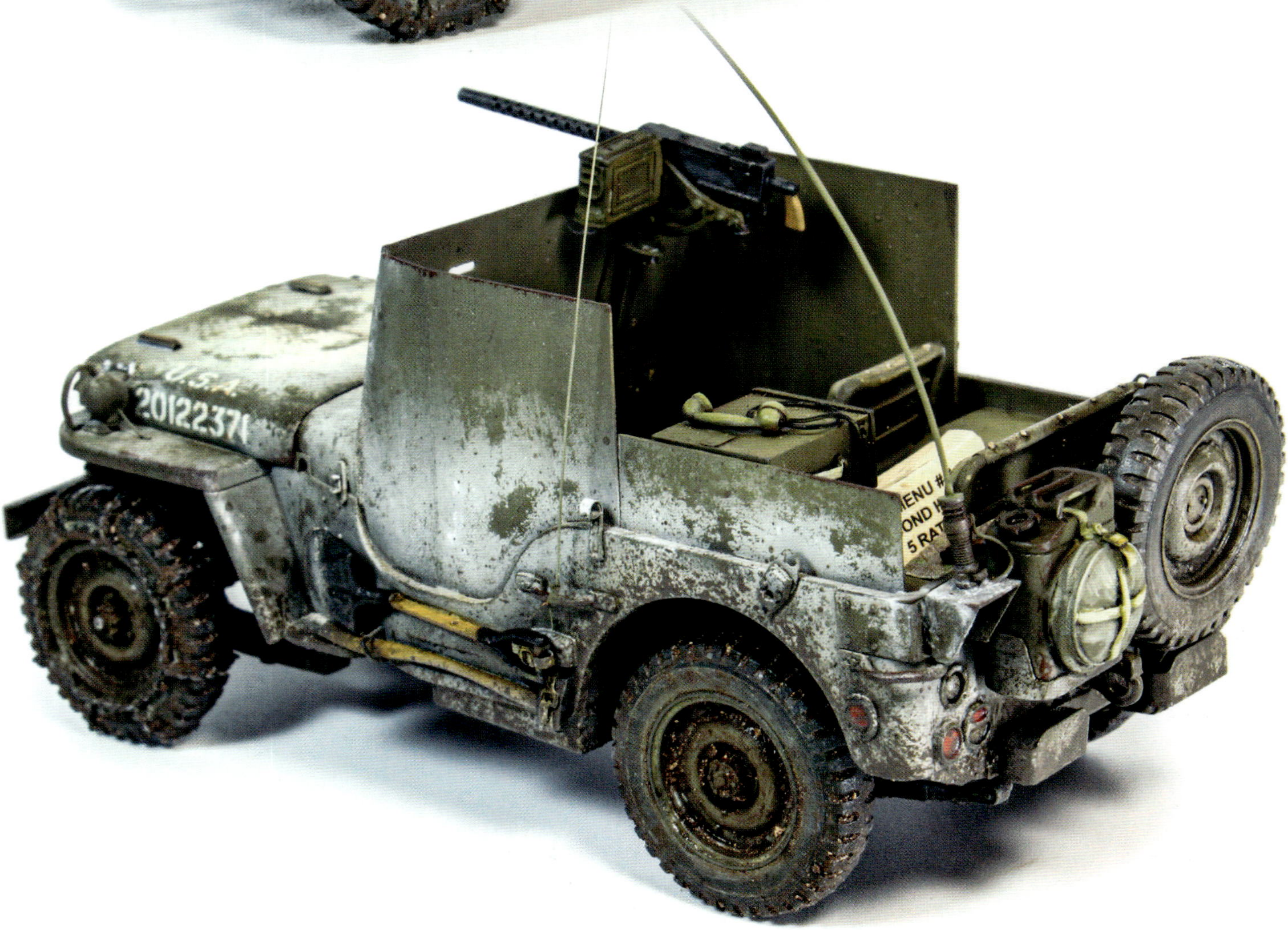
U.S.A.
20122371

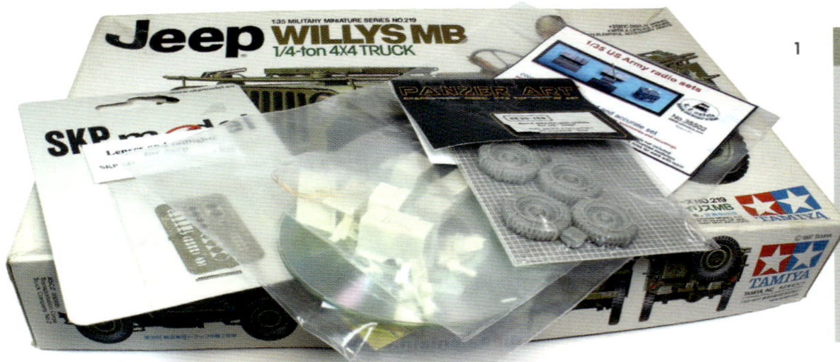

1

MATERIALS USED

- Eduard 35347 "Jeep Willys for Tamiya kit" photo-etch set
- Eduard 35249 "Jeep with armour plates for Tamiya kit" photo-etch set
- Panzer Art 35159 "Road wheels with chains for US Jeep" set
- LZ Models 35502 "US Army radio sets"
- SKP Model 141 "Jeep lenses and tail lights for Tamiya" set
- RB Model 35B082 "7´62 mm Browning M1919" set

1 This good quality kit belongs to the Japanese company Tamiya and has the reference code 35219. The kit is simple, but detailed and with perfect fittings, and can be highly recommended if you want to have fun building a model which is not too complicated. However, some small omissions of obvious details do make one wonder why such an important company as Tamiya has not taken more care of items such as the missing driver's pedals and the characteristic hooks of the hood. But in any case, like any other model kit, this one can be upgraded ad infinitem, it all depends on what we want to achieve.

2

3

4

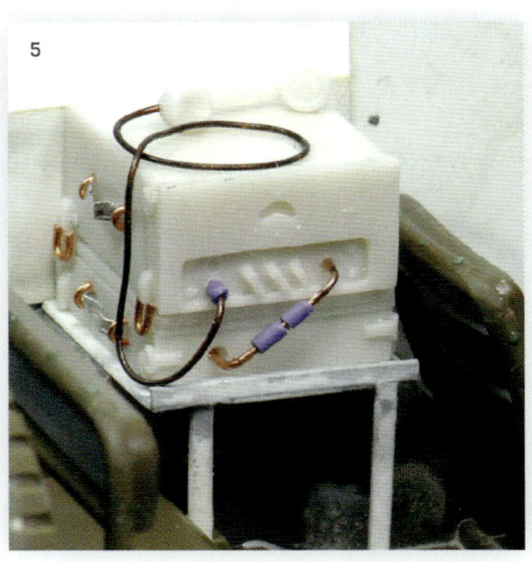

5

6

2 The front wheels were replaced with new resin wheels that include the snow chains.

3 In the back, the frame and antenna for the radio received more details.

4 Straps and supports were added for the tools.

5 The radio table was built with plastic. The radio comes from the LZ Models set.

6 The back part of the seats was detailed by adding the structure and the hooks for the canvas covers of the seats.

7 The driver's pedals were built with plastic and photo-etched parts.

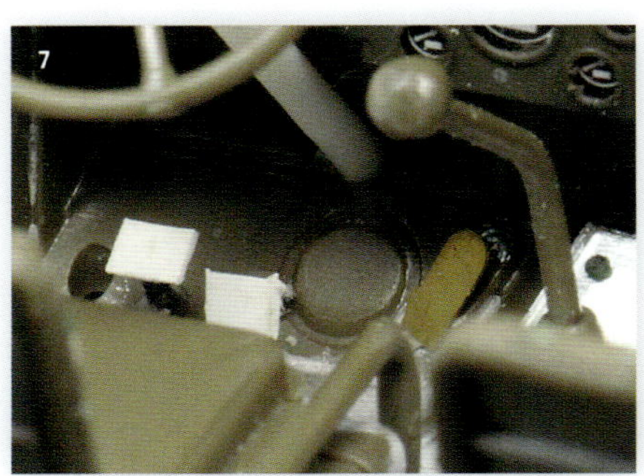

7

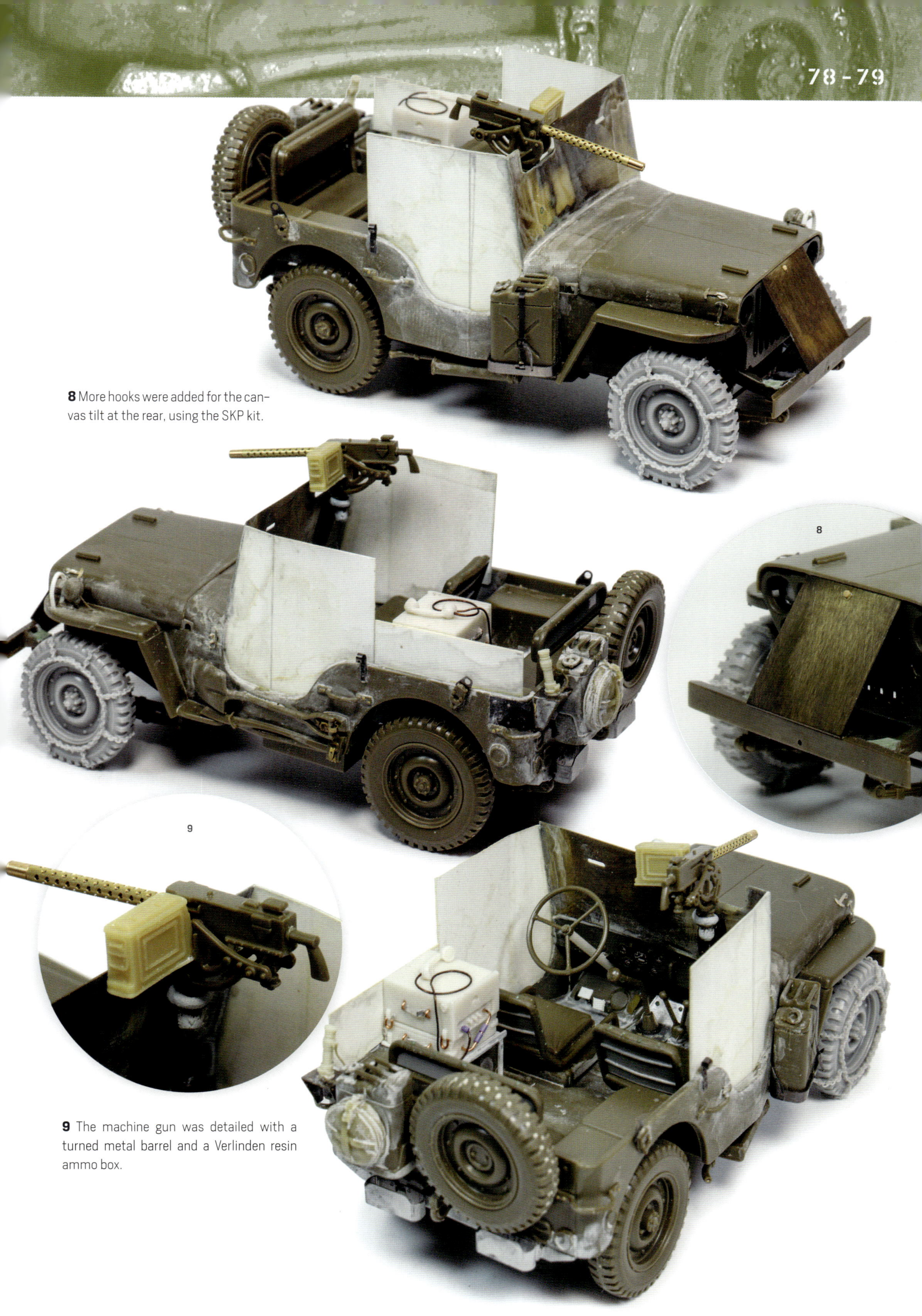

8 More hooks were added for the canvas tilt at the rear, using the SKP kit.

9 The machine gun was detailed with a turned metal barrel and a Verlinden resin ammo box.

10 A basecoat was airbrushed with the color US Olive Drab 71.043.

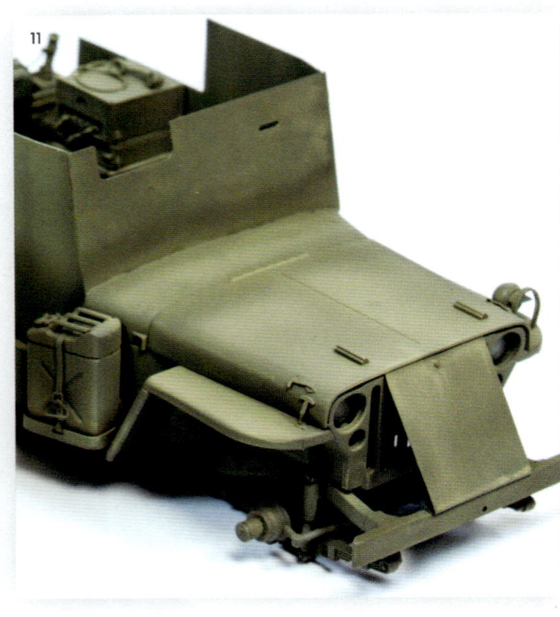

11 Next some highlights were added, very subtly, with Beige 71.074, also with the airbrush.

12 Interior parts received some dirt and mud residues using the pigments Light Sienna 73.104 and Light Slate Grey 73.113.

13 Damp and grease effects were added with the Weathering Effects products designed especially for this purpose, Petrol Spills 73.817 and Wet Effects 73.828.

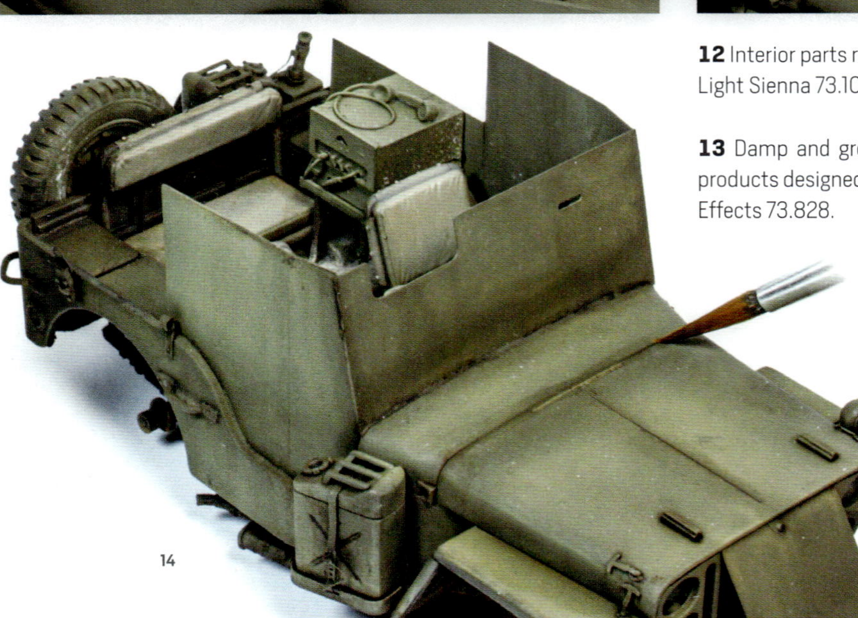

14 Details and recesses were outlined with Dark Brown Wash 76.514.

WHEELS

15 The wheels were first painted with the same basecoat of OD and, later on, the tire was painted with Black 71.073, using a brush.

16 A ring around the tire was airbrushed with Dark Rubber 70.306.

17 Washes are applied with Iraqi Sand 70.819, thinned with water in a 95% proportion and with a touch of soap to break the surface tension

18 For the following mud effects, we used Burnt Umber 73.110 and Dark Yellow Ochre 73.103 pigments, fine sand and Acrylic Gloss Gel.

19 The pigments were mixed until a thick consistency was obtained.

20 This mix was applied on the wheel and the excess was removed afterwards with a damp cloth.

21 Using the airbrush, some Polyurethane Gloss Varnish 26.650 was sprayed over the driving surface of the tire.

22 The wheels are finished with the application of Rain Marks 73.819 a small brush was used to draw some radial lines to simulate the stains of dirty water.

23 The decals were fixed with Decal Fix 73.213 and Decal Softener 73.212 over a surface previously airbrushed with Polyurethane Gloss Varnish 26.650.

24 The next part was the camouflage, at first spraying some hairspray over the whole external surface of the jeep.

25 With the airbrush, a thin coat of White 70.951 is sprayed over the external surface.

26 After some minutes, the painted surface is dampened with warm water and scratched – using a hard sable brush – in order to remove bits of the color. These typical scratches can be created also by passing a toothpick over the surface.

27 Surface details are outlined again with a mix of Burnt Umber and Black oils, thinned in a 90% proportion with White Spirit.

28 A poster is added to customize the vehicle – for this, some period pin-up pictures in photo paper were scaled down and printed.

29 The picture needed was cut out and its thickness was reduced by sanding the back with thin grain sandpaper.

30 With a bit of vinyl glue, the picture was fixed in the desired position.

31 Using some Flat Red 70.957, a red cross was painted on another can in order to differentiate its content.

32 Using small applications of white oil paint, more effects are created over the white camouflaged surface.

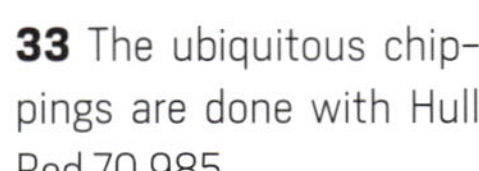

33 The ubiquitous chippings are done with Hull Red 70.985.

34 With a pencil, the polished areas are created where the metal is visible.

35 Using Stone Grey 70.884, first pure and later mixed with some Chocolate Brown 70.872 and Polyurethane Gloss Varnish 26.650, some splashes are simulated on the lower part of the vehicle.

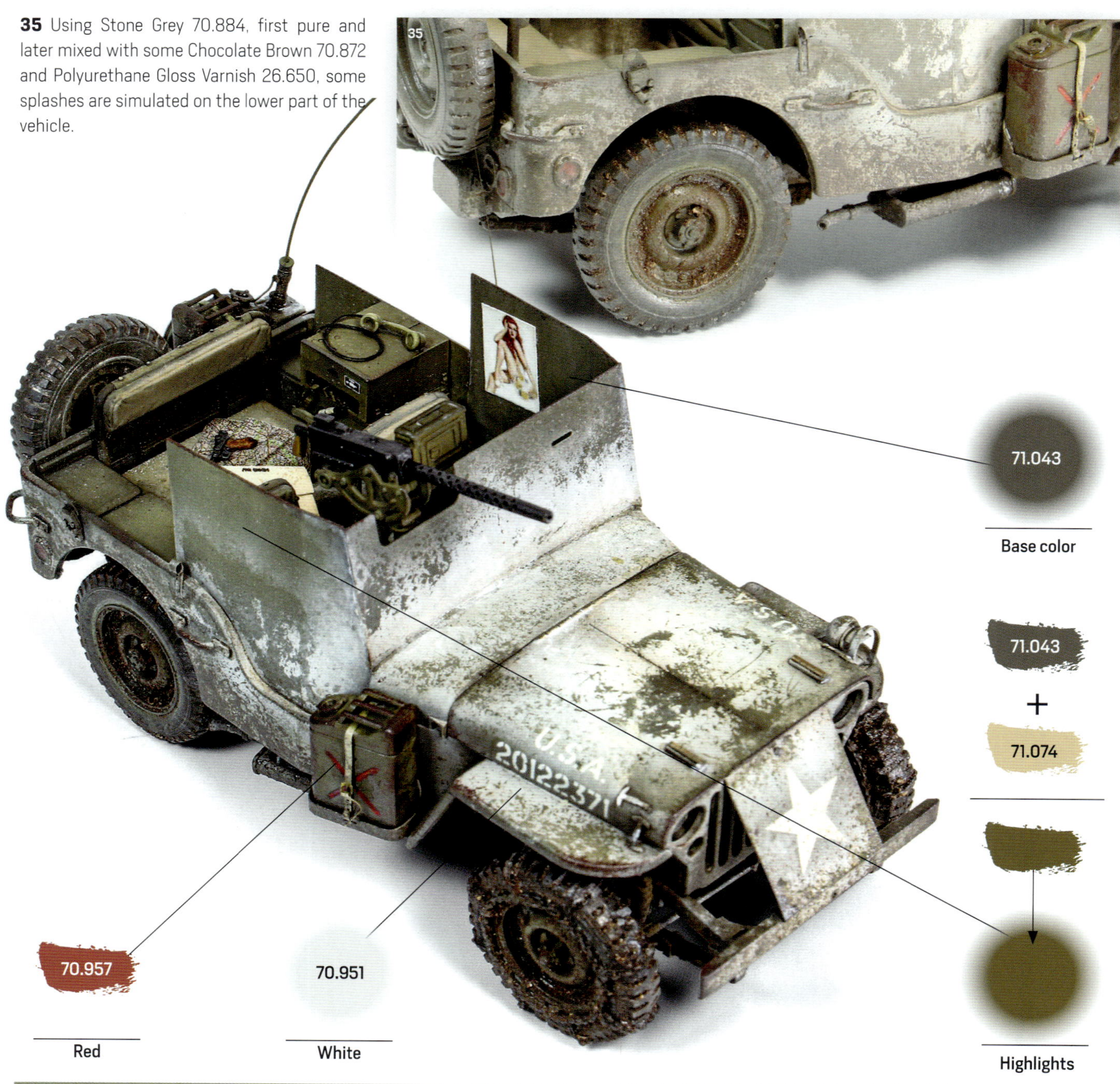

CAMOUFLAGE

COLOR CHART

Camouflage:
Base color:
US Olive Drab 71.043
Highlights:
US Olive Drab 71.043
Beige 71.074
White: White 70.951
Red: Flat Red 70.957

Wheels:
Base:
US Olive Drab 71.043
Tire base:
Black 71.073
Dust:
Dark Rubber 70.306
Wash:
Iraqi Sand 70.819
Mud effects:
Burnt Umber 73.110
Dark Yellow Ochre 73.103
Transparent Water 26.201
Gloss Varnish 26.650
Rain Marks 73.819

Weathering:
Dirt & mud:
Light Sienna 73.104
Light Slate Grey 73.113
Oil & grease:
Petrol Spills 73.817
Wet Effects 73.828
Wash:
Dark Brown 76.514
Chipping:
Hull Red 70.985
Pencil

Splashes:
Stone Grey 70.884
Chocolate Brown 70.872
Polyurethane Gloss Varnish 26.650

Decals:
Polyurethane Gloss Varnish 26.650
Decal Fix 73.213
Decal Softener 73.212

WEATHERING

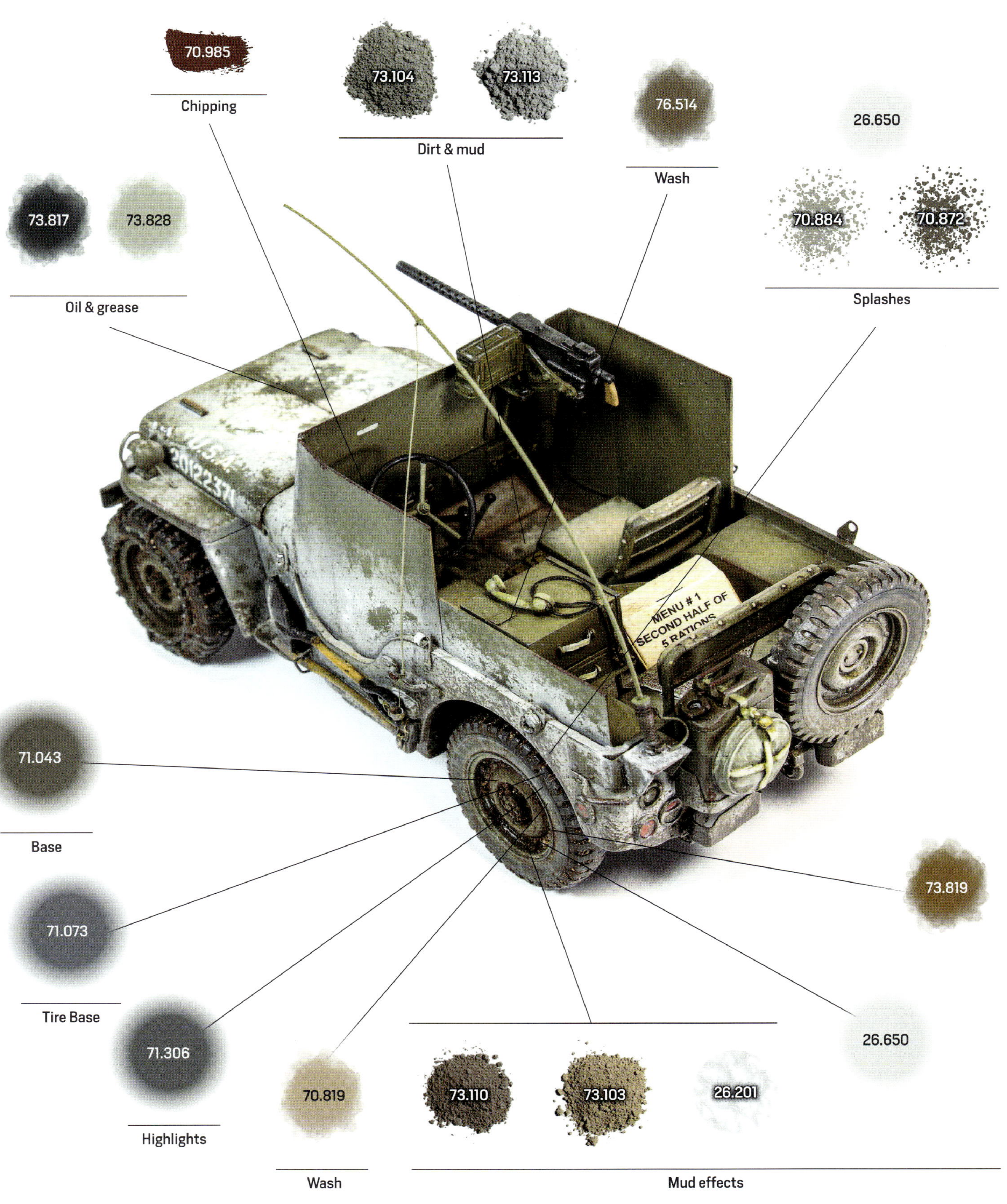

WHEELS

SHERMAN M4A3 USMC

IWO JIMA, 1945

The camouflage patterns used by the US Marine Corps were, most of the time, the result of an effort of improvisation by the crews. Until 1945 there was no regulation about camouflage schemes and colors or about their distribution. All vehicles had to be painted in Sand No 3 FS30277/5C3 with patches of Earth Red No 8 FS30117/7E6, Black No 10 FS37038 and Forest Green No 11 FS 34079/30F4, even if many of them kept using the last color as a base color.

In Iwo Jima the Marines found a setting that once again left the actual camouflage completely out of context. The island consisted of ravines, valleys, cliffs and hills. In different points of the island, sulphuric vapor escaped through cracks in the terrain. The dry earth only supported crude grass and meagre trees and there was no drinkable water. The land was formed by volcanic rock and a thick layer of sand and black ashes with metallic reflections. The contrast between this sand and the US tanks painted in Sand No. 3 gave the Japanese some excellent targets for their new 47 mm type 1 anti-tank guns. That fact, added to the countless mines deployed on the island, caused a 50% casualty rate among the tanks of the 4th and 5th Marine Divisions, and forced the 3rd Marine Division, which was held in reserve, to enter combat before the day was over.

On February 19th 1945, the invasion of the beaches in the north of the island started. Tacticians had estimated the duration of the operation in five days. But the US flag didn't fly over the whole island until March 26th, after the Americans had paid the highest price of the whole Pacific campaign, 6.766 casualties and almost 20.000 wounded. For the Japanese, losing Iwo Jima was an irredeemable disaster. They had lost a portion of their nation, and in its defense had sacrificed more than 21.000 lives.

The 5th Marine Tank Battalion was part of the 5th Marine Division in Iwo Jima. Their Sherman tanks were different from the rest in that they did not have any extra armour at the front. On the sides of the hull, they had installed oak planks and the gap between these and the hull was filled with concrete. In order to avoid access by the suicidal Japanese anti-tank teams, the Marines inserted sharp cut-out strips of tin on the upper edge of the planks. On the sides of the turret, they placed spare track links with the guide tooth facing outward. The running gear was covered with planks to prevent the Japanese, loaded with hand grenades, from throwing themselves under the tanks in an attempt to immobilize the vehicle.

To protect the most vulnerable areas, like hatches, periscopes and fans from anti-tank charges, the crews welded nails, pointing up, to the surface. Because of this, the Sherman tanks of the 5th Marine Tank Battalion were nicknamed "Hedgehogs". This unit identified their tanks using tactical numbers inside white squares in the front, under the machine-gun and on the sides.

COLOR EQUIVALENCE CHART

USMC	Federal Standard	Model Air
Sand No. 3	FS30277 5C3	71.244 Sand Beige
Earth Red No.8	FS30117 7EG	71.293 US Earth Red
Black No.10	FS37038	71.057 Black
Forest Green No.11	FS34079 30F4	71.294 US Forest Green

SHERMAN M4A3 USMC

In order to portray a "Hedgehog" from the 5th Marine Tank Battalion in Iwo Jima, Tamiya's Sherman model M4A3, reference 35250, was used, a re-release of the older kit from 1981. Even considering its age, the model stands the test of time quite decently, but it obviously cannot compete with the modern kits. Still, for the kind of work we want to do, it fits perfectly.

MATERIALS USED

- Verlinden 388 "PSP Plating" set
- M4 Models 35006 "Ruedas Sherman" set
- Jordi Rubio TG-17 "US 75 mm Tank Gun M3"
- RB Model 35B082 "7,62 mm Browning M1919" kit
- Grand Line 12,70 mm 1/2" Hex Nut set

1 For the plank side armor, ice-cream sticks were used, properly adapted to the shape of the tank, and for the protection of the running gear, balsa wood, normally used for naval modelling.

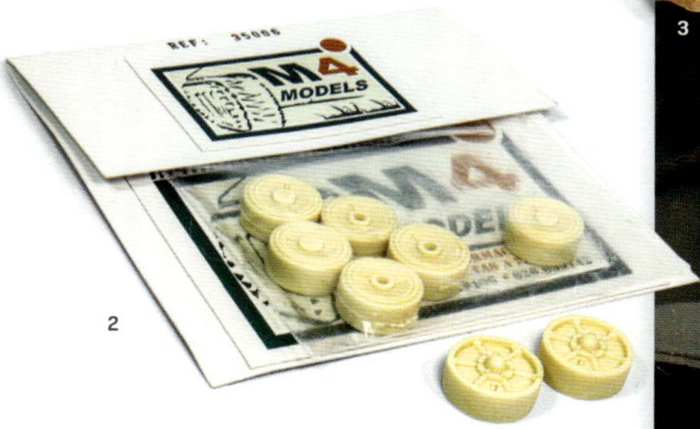

2 The idler wheels were replaced with better resin ones from M4 Models.

3 To fix the support nuts on the planks, some small holes were drilled and a Grand Line nut inserted in the gap.

4 These were affixed to the wood with cyanoacrylate glue.

5-6 To simulate the concrete in the gap between the planks and the hull, Magic Sculpt bi-component putty was used. This mixture was inserted in the gap and the concrete texture was added with a hard bristle brush.

7 The 25-gallon drum was made using an Italeri drum, which was sanded, removing all its detail and rounding the corners. The straps are made of tin foil and the lid came from a jerry can.

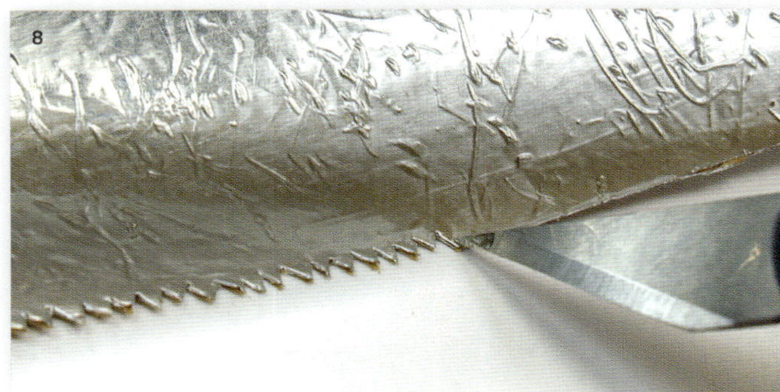

8 Aluminum foil and a sharp knife were used to simulate the cut out tin strips.

9 To simulate the nails, holes were drilled and in them a length of copper wire was glued.

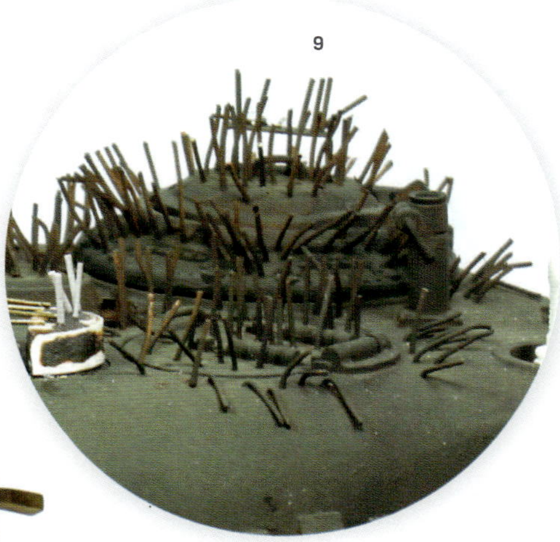

9

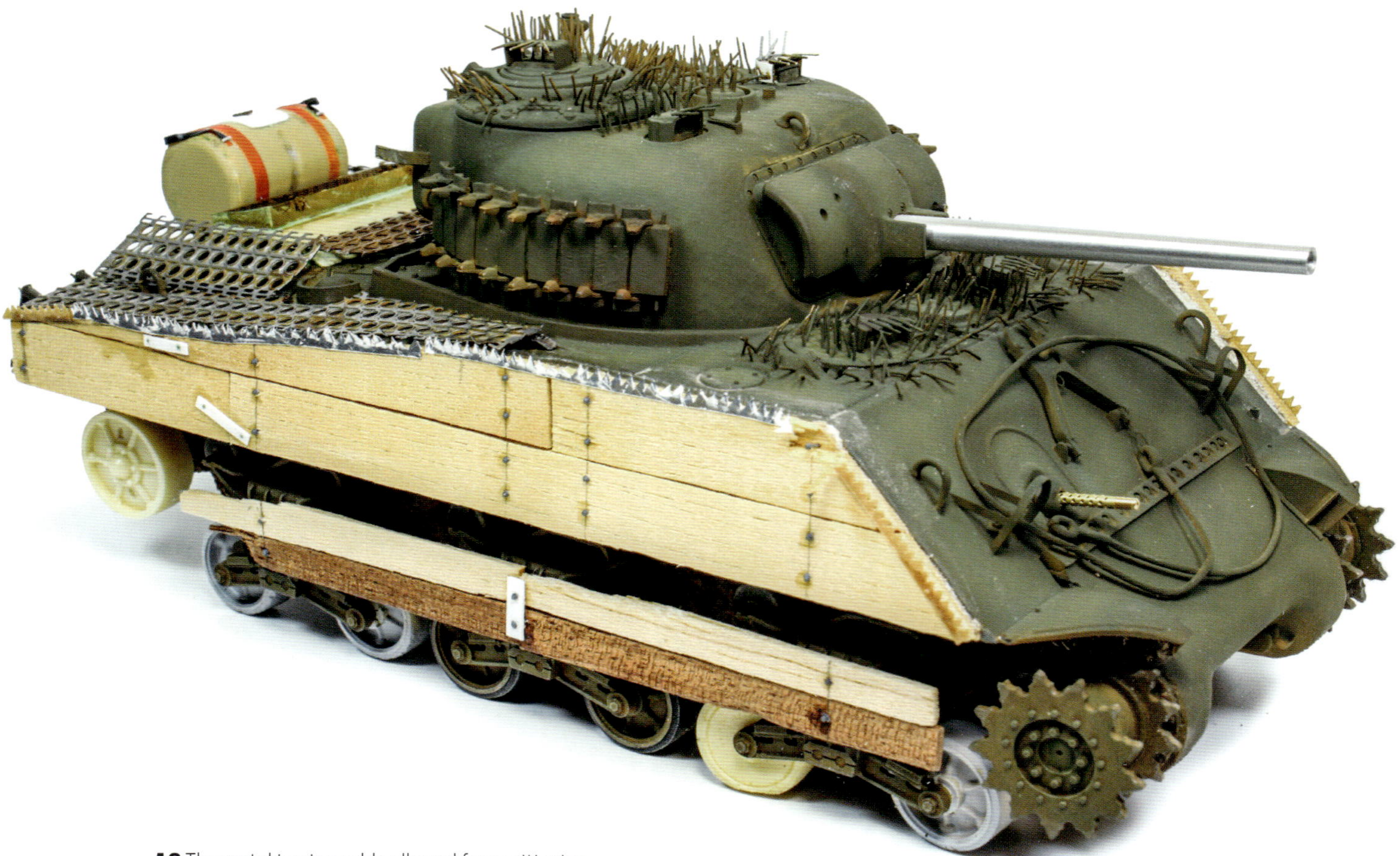

10 The metal towing cable allowed for positioning it in a natural and convincing way.

10

11 Painting started with application of the FS34079 green tone, airbrushing US Forest Green 71.294 in thin coats to cover the complete model.

12 The sides were also painted with an airbrush, using Camouflage Sandbeige RAL 1039 71.244 to simulate the color Sand No 3.

13 Using masking tape, a template was created to outline and place the different tones which compose the camouflage.

14 The masks were positioned and the right color was applied everywhere using the airbrush. As mentioned above, the pattern is composed of Sand Beige 71.244, US Forest Green 71.294, Black 71.057 and US Earth Red 71.293 and the final color was highlighted with a bit of Sand.

13

15 Some Ocean Gray 71.273 was airbrushed over the cut-out tin strips.

16 The mask was removed and the tin basecoat was revealed.

17 The PSP plating was painted with a brush, using a mix of Orange Brown 70.981 and Chocolate Brown 70.872.

18 Next, a wash was applied with Light Rust Wash 76.505.

19 Once dry, another wash was applied on the same area, this time with Orange Rust 71.130.

20 In the green areas of the hull and the turret, a filter was applied with Dark Yellow Wash 76.503.

21 Using sepia oil paint thinned in a 90% proportion with white spirit the reliefs and recesses were outlined.

22 With some heavily thinned Beige 71.074, small areas were airbrushed where dust and dirt would have accumulated.

23 The decals were applied following the usual procedure: first some Decal Fix 73.213 was brushed unto the surface, next the decal was placed on the correct area and finally Decal Medium 73.212 was applied to soften the decal so that it would adapt perfectly to the surface.

24 With a bit of Light Rust 70.301, some rusted chipping was simulated on the reinforcement bracing plates of the planks.

25 The glasses of the periscope were painted in a blue-green tone and varnished with Polyurethane Gloss Varnish 26.650.

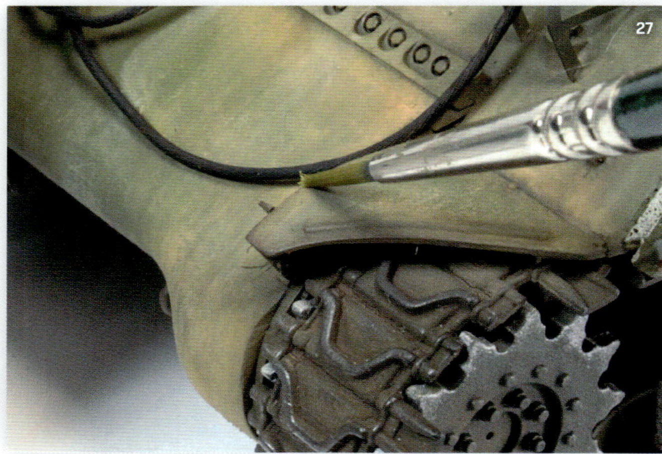

26 Some selected chipping was applied with the sponge technique using Dark Rust 70.302.

27 In other areas, these effects were created by using a brush.

28 The metallic effects are very convincing if done with a graphite bar and a blending stump.

29 The dust effects are simulated with the with Light Slate Grey 73.113 and Light Yellow Ochre 73.102 pigments, fixed to the surface with Airbrush Thinner 71.061.

29

DIRT & GRASS

30 Some dirt and mud residues, created with pigments and plaster, were added.

31 For the dry grass, natural plants were used.

32 These were placed in the areas considered appropriate.

33 The same procedure was followed with the earth.

34 The lid of the water drum was covered with Liquid Mask 70.523.

35 And airbrushed with some Wet Effects 73.828.

36 Once the airbrush work was finished, the mask was removed.

34 The exhaust was painted with Chocolate Brown 70.872 and Light Rust Wash 70.301.

35 The spilt oil was painted with Fuel Stains 73.814 from the Weathering Effects range.

36 The soot typically found on exhaust pipes was created with some Black Smoke 73.116 pigment applied dry.

37 To finish, some splashes with Engine Grime 73.815 were added.

15

SHERMAN M4A3 USMC

WEATHERING

COLOR CHART

Camouflage:
Base color:
US Forest Green 71.294
Sand:
Sand Beige 71.244
Brown:
US Earth Red 71.293
Black:
Black 71.057
Dented tip stripes:
Ocean Gray 71.273

Mask:
Liquid Mask 70.523

Exhaust:
Chocolate Brown 70.872
Light Rust 76.505
Outline:
Sepia (oil)

Periscopes:
German Green Tail Light 70.308
Periscopes 70.309

Weathering:
Dust:
Beige 71.074
Light Yellow Ochre 73.102
Airbrush Thinner 71.061

Rust:
Light Rust 70.301
Chipping:
Dark Rust 70.302
Metallic effects:
Graphite bar & blending stump
Water effects:
Wet Effects 73.828
Oil & grease:
Fuel Stains 73.814
Engine Grime 73.815
Black Smoke 73.116

PSP plating:
Base color:
Orange Brown 70.981
Chocolate Brown 70.872
Wash:
Light Rust 76.505
Orange Rust 71.130

Decals:
Decal Fix 73.213
Decal Softener 73.212

PERISCOPES
70.309
+
70.308
PSP PLATING
Base color
70.981
+
70.872
Washes
76.505
71.130
71.273
Dented tip stripes:
71.294
Base color
71.293
Brown
71.244
Sand
71.057
Black

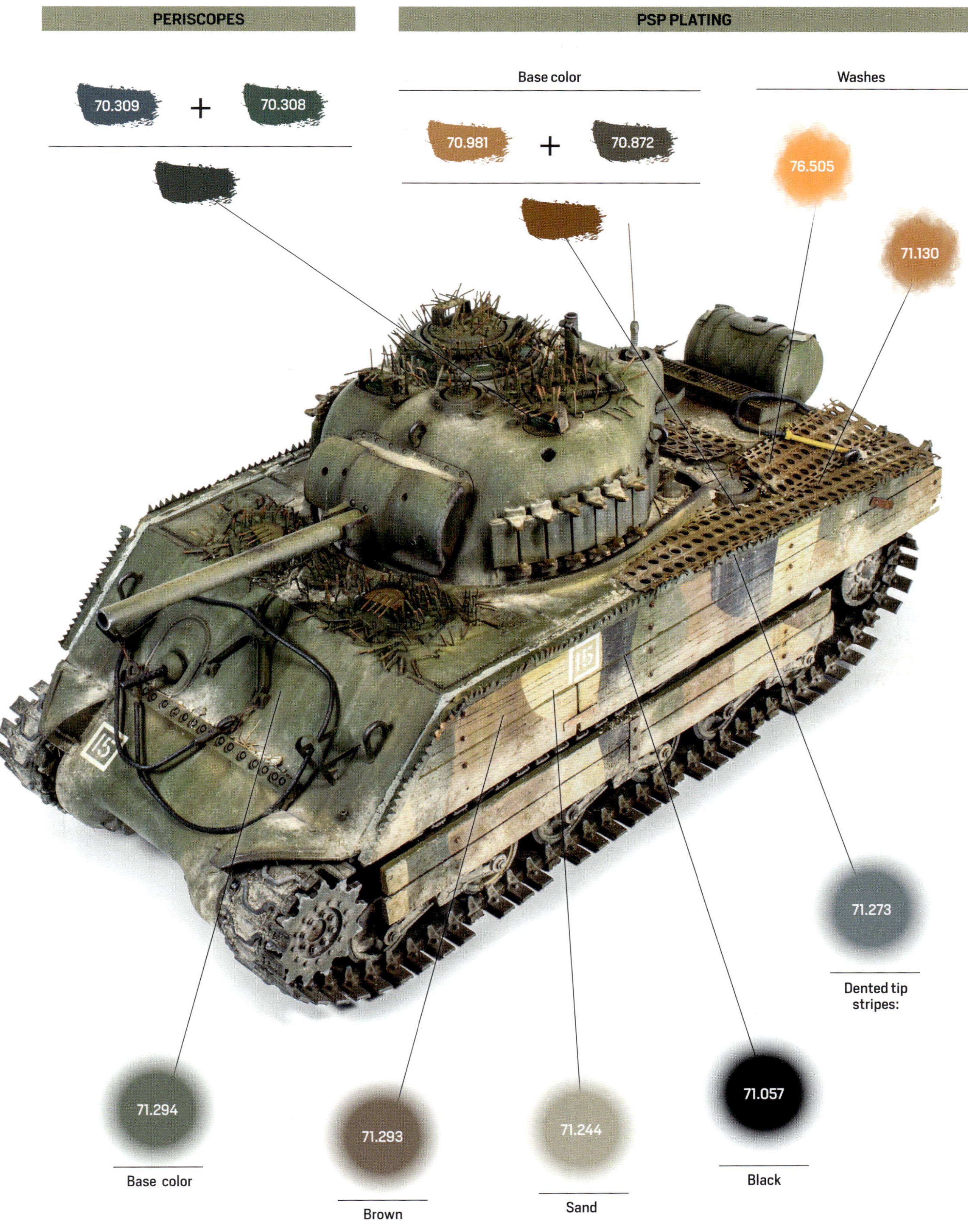

CAMOUFLAGE

SHERMAN M4A3 76 W

SOMMERFELD, GERMANY, 1945

COLOR EQUIVALENCE CHART

US Army	Federal Standard	Model Air
Light Green No. 1	FS34151 30E8	71.137 US Light Green
Earth Red No.8	FS30117 7EG	71.293 US Earth Red
Black No.10	FS37038	71.057 Black
Olive Drab No.9	FS34087 4F4	71.043 US Olive Drab

Following the introduction of the Sherman tank M4A1 (76), it was apparent that the split gunner's hatch couldn't be opened without interfering with the operation of the 50 caliber machine gun. In order to correct this problem and to simplify the original D82081 design of the T23 turret, the Ordnance Department replaced the gunner's hatch with a new one-piece oval-shaped design. This new hatch was bigger and easier to use than those installed in the 75 mm turrets.

An Ordnance Department report from June 1944 reported that the new hatch would be present in all M4A1 (76) tanks built after August 1st, and in all the M4A3 (76) after August 15th. This objective was reached on the M4A1 units, while on the M4A3 (76 model,), which had oval hatches along the factory-installed muzzle brake, the new hatch didn't appear until early 1945.

As of November 1944, the 602nd Engineer Camouflage Battalion, which was located in Northwest Europe in the winter of 1944-1945, started a systematic process of camouflaging the armor of the 12th Army Group. The first designs generally consisted of applying great stripes of Black No. 10, FS37038 or Earth Red No. 8 FS30117/7E6 over the standard Olive Drab No. 9 FS34087/4F4, but sometimes, when additional paints were available, a third tone, No. 1 Light Green FS34151 /30E8, was also used. In that stage of the war, many battalions completely repainted the original white stars on the tanks, leaving no trace of the national insignia.

It is difficult to judge the number of American tanks in northern Europe or Italy that were painted in that camouflage pattern. The black and brown colors are so similar to the olive green in the grey tones of the black and white photographs of the period, that it is mostly impossible to distinguish the individual colors with the exception of a few really sharp images available.

Many tank crews took advantage of the wire mesh fences of the farms and chicken corrals they encountered on their way to Germany: they soldered the fences to the hull and turret of the tanks with a system of steel rods. This created thick frames which easily allowed attaching a natural camouflage of branches which did not need to be affixed with strings or wires. These tanks were called Sommerfield or "Chicken Tanks".

The Sherman tanks were the backbone of the Allied push in Europe. After failing to drive back the Allied armies in the Ardennes Offensive, Germany had no more strength or resources and surrender was just a matter of time, although there still would be hard-fought battles for the final conquest of the German Reich. The huge superiority and determination of the Allies helped them cross the Rhine at Remagen on March 7th 1945, over one of the last bridges still standing, and with this crossing they overcame the last big geographical barrier that prevented the invasion of the Reich.

On April 1st, the Allied forces encircled the Ruhr area and within the Army Group B commanded by Field Marshall Walter Model. On April 25th Soviet and US troops meet at the Elbe River, in the central region of Germany, near Torgau in Northwest Saxony. Yet not until the very moment when the Soviet guns of the advancing Russian troops began bombarding the centre of Berlin did Hitler acknowledge his inevitable defeat.

SHERMAN M4A1

Academy's Sherman M4A3 (76) W "Battle of the Bulge", reference 13500, is a recent release by the Asian company. The kit offers good value, it has quite remarkable details in the molding of the pieces and a complete decal sheet.

MATERIALS USED

- Eduard 35454 "M4A3 Sherman" photo-etch set
- Jordi Rubio 3542 "76 mm M1A1 Sherman M4" set
- RB Model 35B082 "7,62 mm Browning M1919" kit
- Lion Marc LM60005 "1/35 Sherman brass skids with Nuts & Bolts" set

1 To enhance the effect of a laminated steel plate, glue was applied and given texture with a thick-hair brush.

2 In the cast turret, the effect is even more noticeable. For that purpose, Plastic Putty 70.401, was used, applied with a brush. Once dry, it was evened a little more with some gentle sanding.

3 6 Skids 40 Nuts & Bolts (Bogies Not Included)

4

3 To improve the bogies' track skids, the excellent Lion Marc kit was used.

4 The finish was fantastic and true to the scale.

5 The different parts, ready to be primed.

5

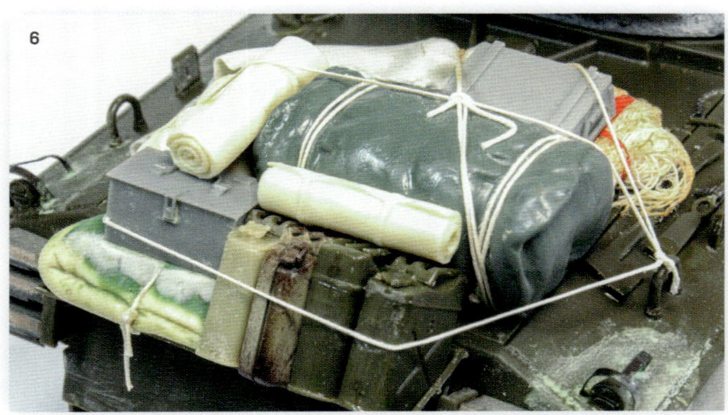

6 The gear was added, composed of spare parts and tied to the vehicle with sewing machine thread.

7 The machinegun was detailed with spares from other kits and the excellent turned cannon from RB.

8 The straps and tool handles were detailed with the photo-etch set by Eduard. Also drain holes were drilled in the oil outlets.

9 The turret was also detailed with photo-etched bits, replacing the plastic handles for some others made of copper wire.

10 The coaxial machinegun on the main gun mantlet was simulated with a piece of brass tube.

11 Finished built model.

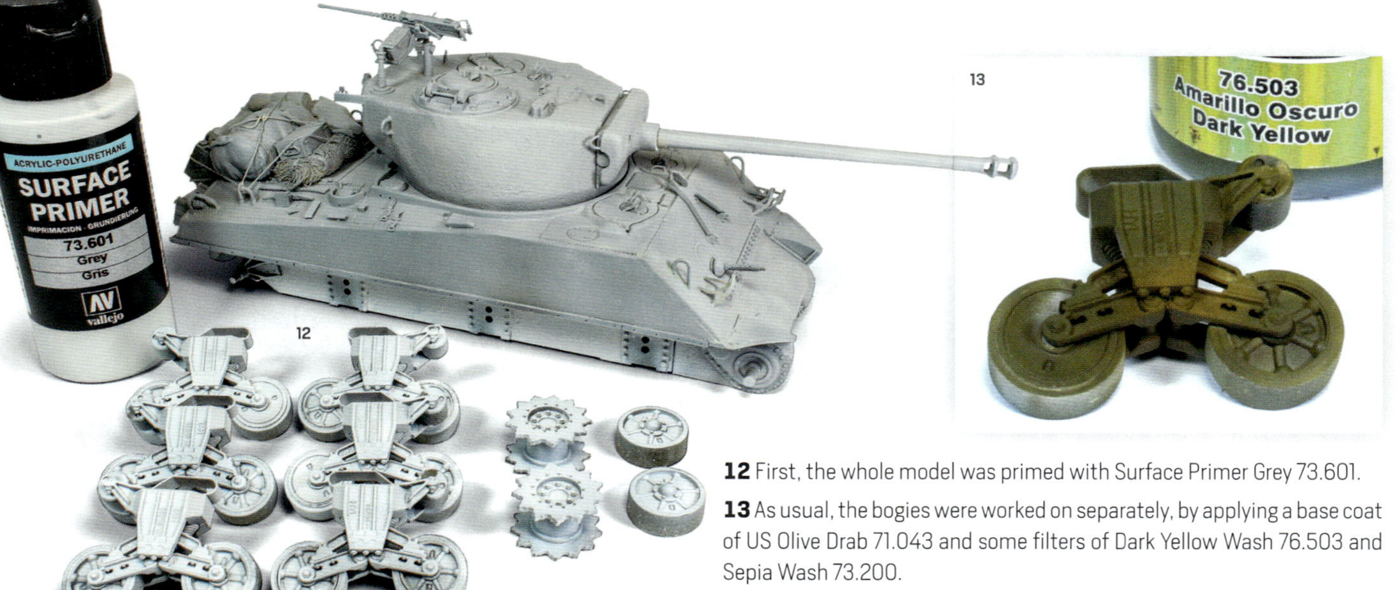

12 First, the whole model was primed with Surface Primer Grey 73.601.

13 As usual, the bogies were worked on separately, by applying a base coat of US Olive Drab 71.043 and some filters of Dark Yellow Wash 76.503 and Sepia Wash 73.200.

14 Over the inner part of the lower side of the hull, Mud and Grass Effect 73.826 from Weathering Effects were applied.

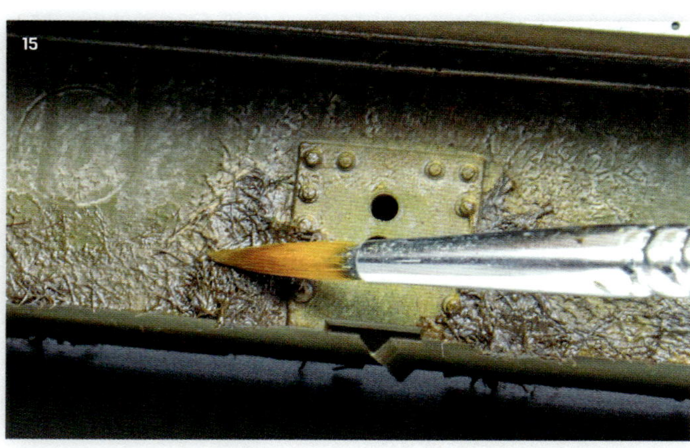

15 Next, a wash was made with European Thick Mud 73.807.

16 The weathering of the lower part was augmented by applying some oils. Small portions of green, yellow, brown and white tones were used.

17 Vertical strokes were blended with a flat brush.

18 Bogies were glued in place and fixed to the tracks.

CAMOUFLAGE

19 Now it was the right time to apply the basecoat of US Olive Drab 71.043 over the whole upper part of the tank.

20 Using a template, the camouflage scheme was reproduced. The third shade was applied first, using US Light Green 71.137, applied with the airbrush at low pressure to avoid detaching the masks by mistake.

21 The same was done with the next color of the camouflage, Black 71.057.

22 Each color was highlighted by using Beige 71.074 for the olive drab, Panzer Grey 71.056 for the black tone and a mix of Eau de Nil Duck Egg Green 71.009 and White 71.270 for the light green.

23

23 The main details were outlined and shaded with a mix of black and burnt umber oils thinned in a 90% proportion with white spirit.

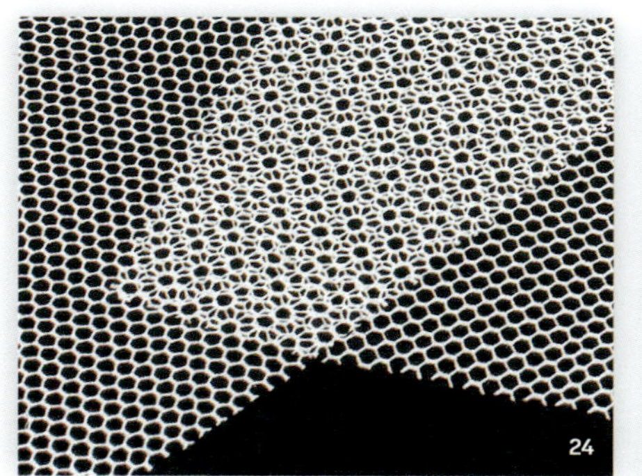

24

25

24 - 25 To simulate the "chicken wire" a bit of tulle fabric mesh was used. Each piece was cut out with the use of some previously designed templates.

26 The pieces were airbrushed with Rust 71.080.

26

27 The steel rods that were soldered over the Sherman hull were simulated with copper wire.

28 Washes were applied over the rods with Sepia 73.200 and Desert Dust 76.522.

29 Using various oil colors, a general weathering was applied over the vehicle, working area by area, placing small portions of oils over the surface previously dampened with thinner.

30 With a brush, the colors were blended until some subtle transparencies were achieved.

31 The mask was removed to get the effect of the bare metal on the cannon, caused by the recoil.

32 The net was glued on the rods using cyanoacrylate glue

33 With a bit of tin foil, characteristic air-recognition panels was made. These panels changed color depending on the orders for the day.

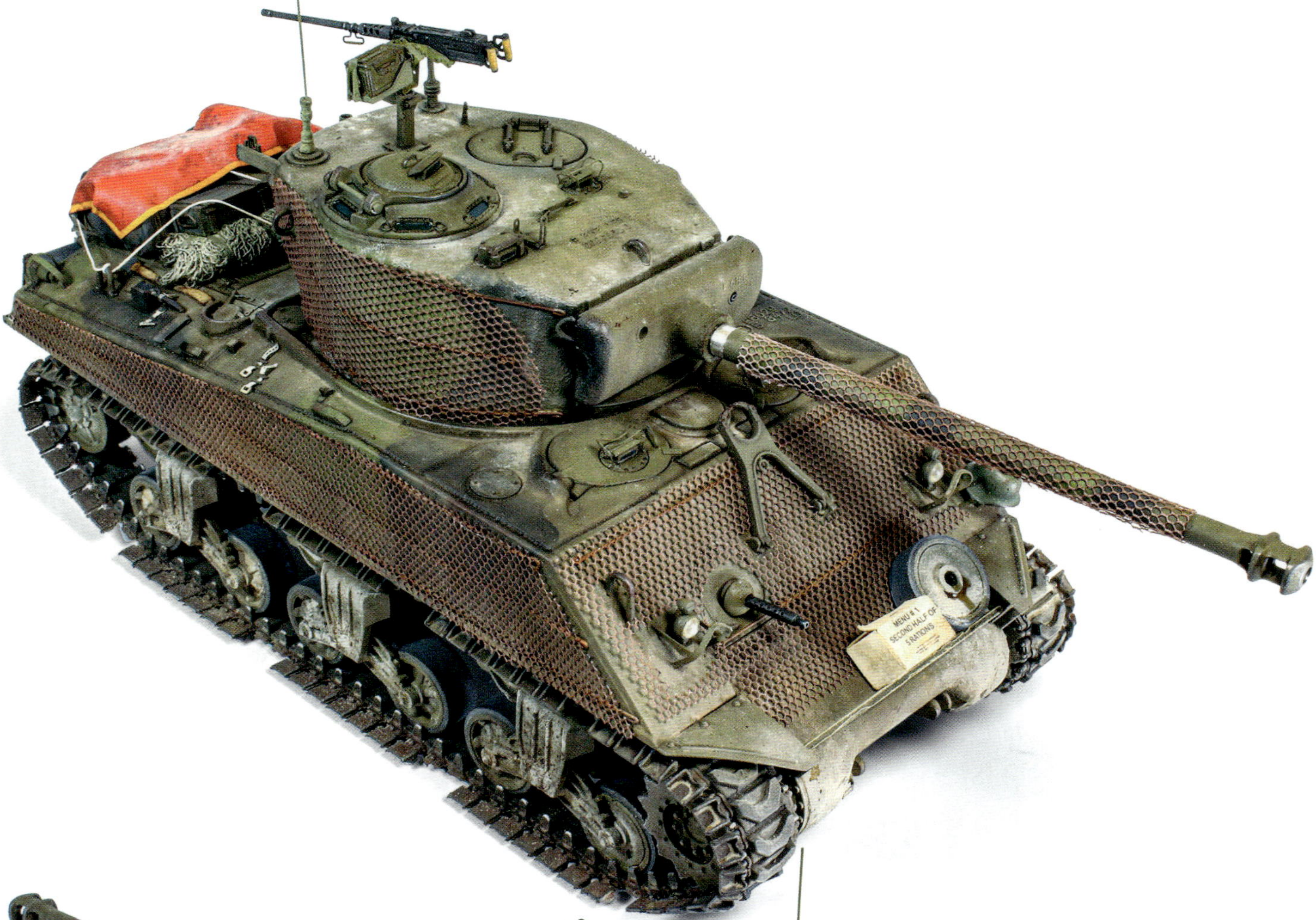
MENU # 1
SECOND HALF OF
5 RATIONS

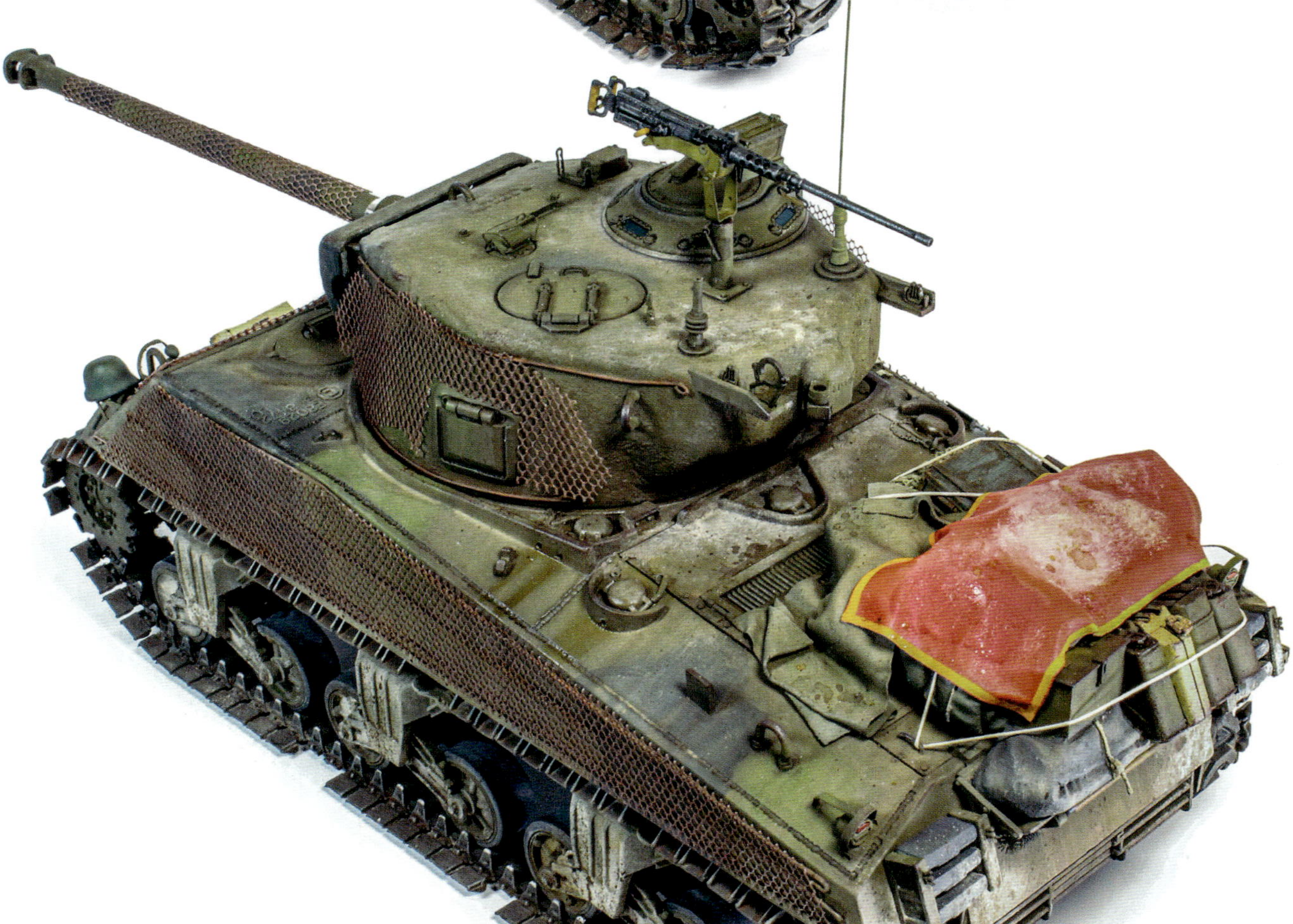

SHERMAN M4A1

COLOR CHART:

Camouflage:
Priming:
Grey 73.601
Turret base color:
US Olive Drab 71.043
Turret highlights:
Beige 71.074
Hull base color:
US Light Green 71.137

Hull highlights:
Eau de Nil "D. E. Green" 71.009
Off-White 71.270
Camouflage base color:
Black 71.057
Camouflage highlights:
Panzer Grey 71.056
Shadows (oils):
Black
Burnt Umber

Steel rods:
Washes:
Sepia 73.200
Desert Dust 76.522

Air-recognition panel:
Signal Red 71. 070
Orange X-6 (Tamiya)

Chicken wire:
Rust 71.080

Weathering:
Lower hull:
Mud and Grass Effect 73.826
European Thick Mud 73.807

73.601
Priming
71.043
Turret base color
71.074
Turret highlights
71.137
Hull base color
71.009 + 71.270
Hull highlights
71.057
Camouflage base color
71.056
Camouflage highlights

CAMOUFLAGE

WWII US ARMY
PROFILES GALLERY

M4A2 "Condor" US Marines Tarawa, Gilbert Islands . November 1943. **Model Air** 71.137, 71.289, 71.138, **Model Color** 70.857.

M4A1 "Sloppy Joe" (76) W US Army, 603 rd. STC Dutch New Guinea, March 1944. **Model Air** 71.137, 71.289, 71.303, 71.043.

M4A3 (76) W T26 turret US Army, near Riedwihr, France 1945. **Model Air** 71.289, 71.006, 71.043, 71.001.

M4A3 "Applejack" US Marines, 4[Th] Tank Battalion A Company, Iwo Jima. **Model Air** 71,057, 71.007, 71.293, 71.043, 71.137, 71.075.

M4A1 US Army, 1st Armored Division, Tunisia 1943. **Model Air** 71.303, 71.289, 71.043, 71.138, 71.075.

M10 White broad bands pattern, US Army, Italy 1945. **Model Air** 71.137, 71.289, 71.303, 71.043, 71.001.

Jeep US Marines, Okinawa, April 1945. **Model Air** 71.315, 71.289, 71.138, 71.137, 71.031, 71.077.

Jeep US Army, 60th Infantry Regiment, 9th Division, Bulge, January 1945. **Model Air** 71.315, 71.289, 71.137, 71.031, 71.077.

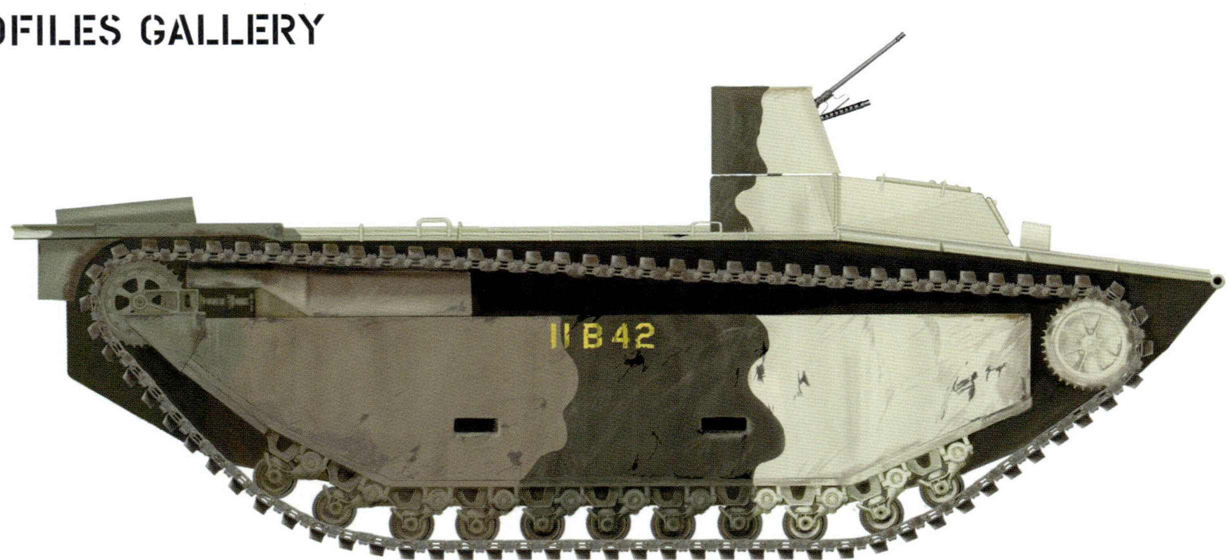

LVT (A) 2 US Marines, unusual Yellow Beach II markings, Iwo Jima, March 1945. **Model Air** 71.057, 71.293, 71.043, 71.137, 71.075.

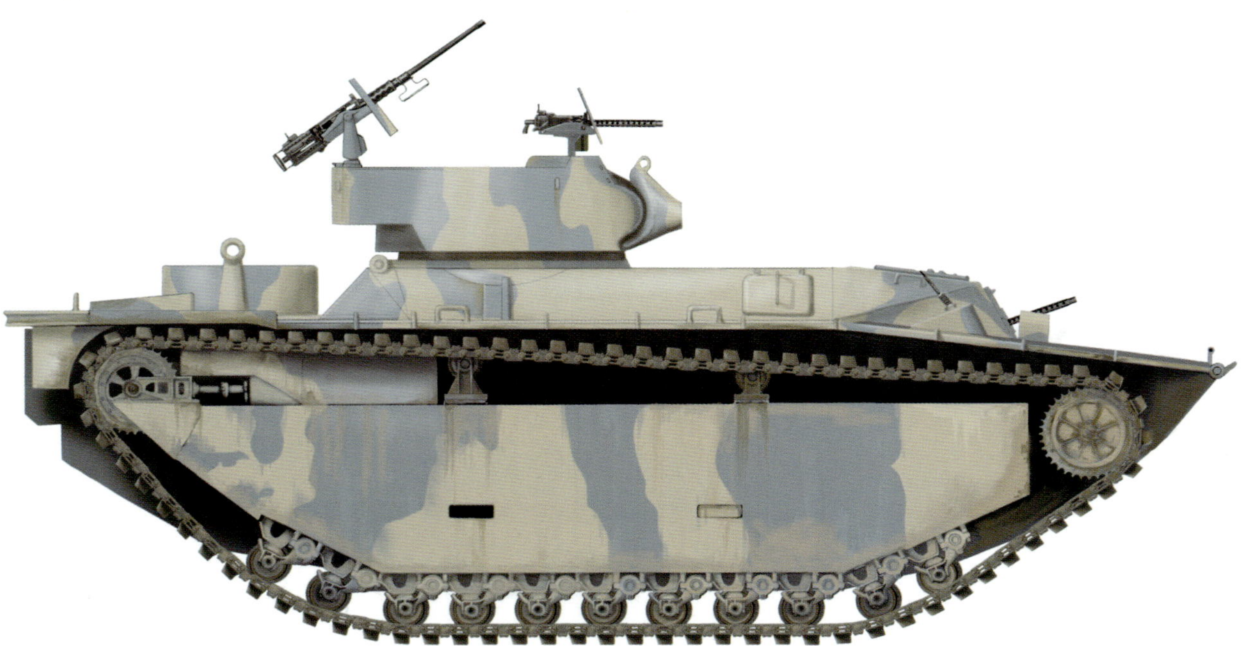

LTV (A) 4 US Marines, 2nd. Armored Amphibian Battalion, Tinian, August 1944. **Model Air** 71.273, 71.132, 71.138.

LVT (A) 1 "Block Buster" US Marines ,Company B, 708th Amphibious Tank Battalion, Saipan, June 1944. **Model Air** 71.273, 71.279, 71.087.

M8 GMC "Scott" Disrupted Pattern, US Army, Italy, Late 1943. **Model Air** 71.289, 71.137, 71.244, 71.132, 71.291.

M5 Stuart "Hothead" US Marines, Namur Island, 1944. **Model Air** 71.289, 71.290, 71.043, 71.132.

WWII US ARMY

PROFILES GALLERY

M29 C Weasel Green scheme, US Marines, Okinawa, May 1945. **Model Air** 71.137, 71.043, 71.289, 71.129.

M29C Weasel Three tones Iwo Jima Camouflage, Iwo Jima, March 1945. **Model Air** 71.007, 71.293, 71.043, 71.137, 71.075, 71.129.

M29 Weasel Mickey Mouse, Flecktarn camouflage, US Army. **Model Air** 71.057, 71.137, 71.007, 71.129, 71.001.

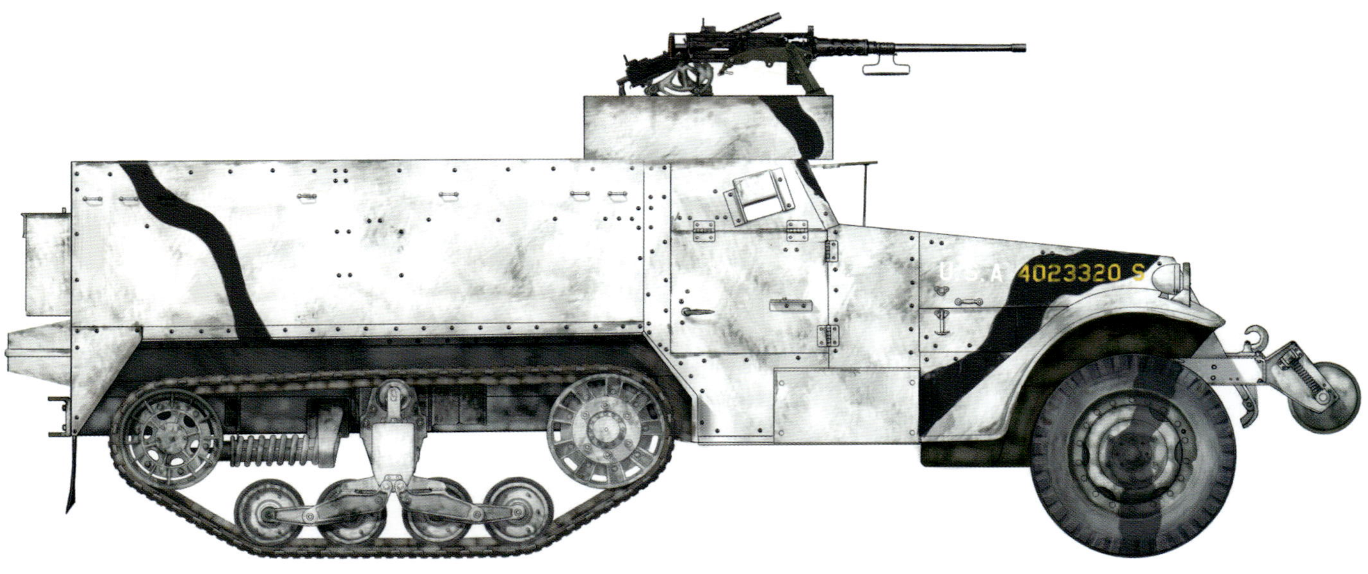

M2A1 Whitewashed camouflage, US Army, Ardennes, 1944. **Model Air** 71.001, 71.013, 71.289, 71.303, 71.315.

M3 75 mm GMC Dark three-tone camo, US Marines, Cape Gloucester, South Pacific, December 1943. **Model Air** 71.040, 71.137, 71.138, 71.135.

M2 US army 3rd Battalion HQ, 67th Armored Regiment, Sicily, July 1943. **Model Air** 71.289, 71.138, 71.132, 71.315.

MODEL GALLERY

BY JAVIER REDONDO

KING KONG
KING
KONG
KING
KONG
ELECTRIC

12
CHAMPAGNE
99

B 37
B37

NITRATO
DE CAL
DE
NORUEGA

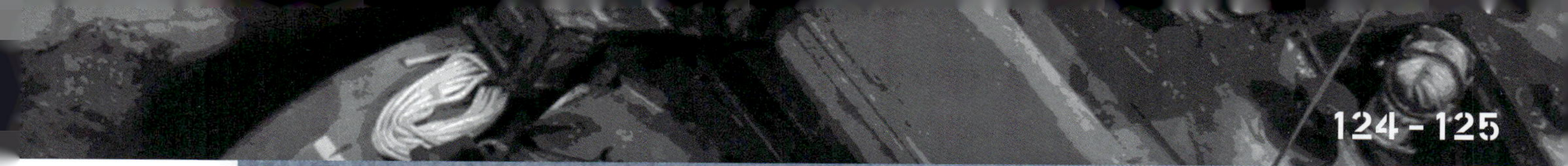

20516267

14

Persil

ЗА
СТАЛИНА!

A CASPE 63 KMS
A BELCHITE 9 KMS

ARMOURED SIDE
Book Series by Vallejo

AV
vallejo